Blind Conceit

Blind Conceit
Politics, Policy and Racial Polarization: Moving Forward to Save America

Star Parker

Sumner Books
Hermosa Beach, CA

Blind Conceit
Politics, Policy and Racial Polarization:
Moving Forward to Save America

Copyright © 2015 Star Parker

FIRST EDITION

Sumner Books

737 3rd St

Hermosa Beach, California 90254

310-337-7003

ISBN 978-1-939104-13-7

CREATORS PUBLISHING

CONTENTS

INTRODUCTION

America at a Crossroads

The Democrats keep telling Americans that Republicans lose national elections because of their conservative brand.

They tell Republicans that if conservatives would just act like liberals -- then maybe, just maybe -- young people and women people, black people and short people, and even perhaps a few illegal people will like them.

They say that if conservatives would just get with the program -- rap a little, smoke a little pot, take off their clothes in front of strangers a little, give up their guns, their God and their disapproval of gays, and, of course, put up only liberal republican candidates for statewide and national seats -- then maybe, just maybe, comedians will stop mocking them and the national news will ignore them instead of trying to destroy them.

Even though mountains of data point to the connection between religion and marriage to civil order, protection of private property and economic prosperity, liberal progressives, in their quest for power, started three wars against our American culture 50 years ago. And it is these three wars, which, over time, collapsed religion and marriage, personal initiative and responsibility, resulting in the stagnated growth of today's American economy.

Yet the answer to the failures of their utopian ideals and public policies is always the same. It's the conservatives' fault, and if the Republicans would rein them in, progressivism would be free to deliver hope and change to guarantee world peace.

The Lie of the Left

Fifty years ago, in order to gain the power to completely transform America into a secular socialist state, liberal progressives began to build a political base by convincing blacks and other low-wage voters that redistribution of wealth was in the interests of social justice.

1

Social justice is the great equalizer. It is meant to level the playing field between the haves and the have-nots; the rich and the poor; the privileged and the underclass; or, as some go as far to say out loud, to take from the sons of the enslavers to give to sons of the enslaved.

Liberals pretend they are against war; however, in their quest for power, they started three wars against our American culture. Unfortunately, blacks were the first group to get caught up in progressive political promises of social justice, thus becoming the first casualties.

For the last 50 years, blacks have been conditioned to put liberal policies and politicians above all other concerns -- above their faith, above their family and above their freedom -- in exchange for so-called social justice.

Please remember that the civil rights movement was a moral movement about removing governmental barriers so blacks could live free according to the constitution. The civil rights generation of the 1950s wanted repentance and revival. The social justice generation of today wants revenge and redistribution, the antithesis of Dr. King's dream.

Progressive War No. 1

War on Religion: weakened our public institutions and opened the door to a culture of corruption.

--1962: Supreme Court struck down state-sponsored school prayer.

--1963: Court ruled cannot read the Bible or recite the Lord's Prayer in public schools.

--1980: Courts ruled to remove Ten Commandments from public schools.

Progressive War No. 2

War on Marriage: weakened women and opened the door to this new culture of meaninglessness.

--Homosexuality is now dividing us and bringing hostility into the public square.

--Abortion has deeply hurt us. (Fifty-six million dead in 40 years should give all of us all great pause.)

--In 1960s, 75 percent of American adults were married, compared with just under 50 percent today.

2

--In 1960s, 45 percent of young adults between 18-24 were marriage compared with just 9 percent today.

--In 1980, when Ronald Reagan was president, 18 percent of births were outside of marriage compared with 43 percent today.

--Blacks: from 22 percent outside of marriage births in the '60s to 72 percent today.

--Whites: from 3 percent outside of marriage births in the '60s to 30 percent today.

--Hispanics: no data in the '60s to 53 percent outside of marriage births today.

In a Gallup poll done earlier this year, 71 percent of respondents between 18 and 34 years old said having a baby outside of marriage is morally acceptable.

According to Ron Haskins of The Brookings Institution, "In 2009, the poverty rate for children in homes with married parents was 11 percent. The poverty rate for children in homes headed by a single mother in that same year was 44.3 percent."

Progressive War No. 3

War on Poverty: weakened family and opened the door to culture of entitlements.

In 2003, I wrote a book called "Uncle Sam's Plantation." I wrote the book to tell my story of what I saw living inside the welfare state and my own transformation.

I talked about government programs like Temporary Assistance for Needy Families, Job Opportunities and Basic Skills Training, Emergency Assistance to Needy Families with Children, section 8 housing and food stamps. A vast sea of perhaps well-intentioned government programs, all initially set into motion in the 1960s, which were going to lift the nation's poor out of poverty.

A benevolent Uncle Sam welcomed mostly poor black Americans onto the government plantation. Those who accepted the invitation switched mindsets from "How do I take care of myself?" to "What do I have to do to stay on the plantation?"

Instead of solving economic problems, government welfare socialism created monstrous moral and spiritual problems. The kind of problems that is inevitable when individuals turn responsibility for their lives over to others. The legacy of American socialism is our blighted inner cities, dysfunctional inner city schools and broken black families.

Through God's grace, I found my way out. It was then that I understood what freedom meant and how great this country is.

I had the privilege of working on welfare reform in 1996, passed by a Republican Congress and signed into law by a Democratic president. A few years after enactment, welfare rolls were down 50 percent.

I thought we were on the road to moving socialism out of our poor black communities and replacing it with wealth-producing American capitalism. So I began to work on promoting school choice so that money would follow the decisions of parents, not an educational establishment controlled by progressive unions. I also worked on personal retirement accounts to replace the government-forced retirement program with wealth-producing opportunities.

But, incredibly, by 2001, we began going in the opposite direction. Power changed political parties, but control stayed in Washington.

Government expanded in many areas, but the biggest affront to my work was the Bush administration's faith-based initiative, a multiple-billion-dollar initiative to put America's churches on welfare.

In 2008, power changed political parties again and, by 2009, instead of poor America relying on socialism becoming more like rich, capitalistic America, rich, capitalistic America started very rapidly becoming more like poor America relying on socialism.

There is some kind of irony that this latest aggressive push for massive government takeover of every aspect of American life is happening under our first black president. When you look into the black community, you cannot help but see the deep damage of liberalism and government control. Yet secularism and socialism seems to be the element of President Barack Obama.

In just 50 years, the stats went from 70 percent of black children being raised by married parents, to 70 percent of black children being raised by a single parent. In just 50 years, blacks went from landowning, entrepreneurial Republicans to government-dependent, reckless Democrats.

The 50-year legacy of liberal progressivism (also known as secular statism) in the black community is that today, 25 percent of blacks wallow in poverty, another 23 percent of blacks work directly for the government, and less than 3 percent of blacks own a business. Black net worth is about $5,000.

And the 50-year legacy of progressive liberal dominance for all cultures is that unmarried adults and low income Americans of all ethnicities have become increasingly liberal leaning and thus government dependent because:

--The War on Religion marginalized personal obligations.

--The War on Marriage marginalized personal commitments.

--And the War on Poverty said someone else will pay the bills for any and all irresponsible behaviors.

Psalm 36:2

"In their blind conceit, they cannot see how wicked they really are." (New Living Translation)

"I'm in this race not just to hold an office, but to gather with you to transform a nation."

Barack Obama

"In their own eyes they flatter themselves too much to detect or hate their sin." (New International Version)

"I don't believe it is possible to transcend race in this country. Race is a factor in this society. The legacy of Jim Crow and slavery has not gone away. It is not an accident that African-Americans experience high crime rates, are poor and have less wealth. It is a direct result of our racial history." -- Barack Obama

"For he flatters himself in his own eyes that his iniquity cannot be found out and hated." (English Standard Version)

"Change will not come if we wait for some other person or some other time. We are the ones we've been waiting for. We are the change that we seek." -- Barack Obama

"For it flatters him in his own eyes concerning the discovery of his iniquity and the hatred of it." (New American Standard Bible)

"I believe marriage is between a man and a woman. I am not in favor of gay marriage. But when you start playing around with constitutions, just to prohibit somebody who cares about another person, it just seems to me that's not what America's about. Usually, our constitutions expand liberties, they don't contract them." -- Barack Obama

"For he flattereth himself in his own eyes, until his iniquity be found to be hateful." (King James Bible)

"I consider it part of my responsibility as president of the United States to fight against negative stereotypes of Islam wherever they appear." -- Barack Obama

5

"They like themselves too much to hate their own sins or even to see them." (Contemporary English Version)

"The point I was making was not that Grandmother harbors any racial animosity. She doesn't. But she is a typical white person. " Barack Obama

Blind Conceit

How can we build a nation of free and prosperous people if we have a nation of irresponsible people that are government dependent?

The liberal progressive social justice lie of the left gripped America's poor and minority communities some 50 years ago and has locked three generations into economic stagnation and dependency on a welfare state.

And, today, progressive liberalism is financially choking our entire society.

In the first three years of the Obama administration, spending on these means-tested programs increased by almost $150 billion, or 31 percent. These welfare programs now cost $900 billion annually, almost a quarter of the budget.

Medicaid, considered one of the three entitlement programs along with Medicare and Social Security, is an additional means-tested poverty program and has a budget of its own at $350 billion in 2013.

Today, Medicaid pays for 53 percent of all births in our country, and it also pays the bills for 60 percent of all long-term nursing homecare. Obamacare qualifies up to 20 million more individuals to the almost 60 million already covered by Medicaid, which is why most Republican governors have rejected to partner with the feds in the tax-funded scheme.

The fact is that the federal government now takes 25 percent of the American economy. In 1980, 20 percent of Americans got more from government then they put in. Today 60 percent of Americans get more from government then they put in.

After 50 years of progressivism dominating our public culture, our public institutions, our public policy and our media, and the last six years of progressive control in the White House, I think it time for the opposition forces to unite energy and tactics to defeat progressivism and reverse the trends of their blind conceit.

This book is my attempt to address six specific topics that I believe conservatives, tea party patriots and maybe even a few Republicans might want to think about going into the 2016 elections.

Part One: The Politics of Race

Part Two: Culture Wars

Part Three: The Disease of D.C.

Part Four: Poverty and Wealth

Part Five: Where We Stand

Part Six: Blind Obedience

In these six parts, you will read a compilation of columns I wrote during my 10 years as a nationally syndicated columnist with Scripps Howard News Service, and the last six months with Morris Communications. I hope within each column you will find insight or ammunition so to not allow progressive liberals to hold our country hostage to their agenda any longer. Out-of-control debt, enslavement to government and broken families are no formula for a great country.

I am convinced that we as a nation are at a critical crossroads -- similar to the 1850s when Abraham Lincoln looked into the Scriptures and quoted the Lord that "a house divided against itself cannot stand" or in the 1960s when Dr. Martin Luther King Jr. looked into the heart of America and said, "Our lives begin to end the day we become silent about things that matter."

My desire is that when you finish reading this book, you also will be convinced that we must together humble progressive liberalism and its Blind Conceit, insuring the next generations of Americans a future and a hope.

First, I want to thank Rick Newcombe at Creators Syndicate for the idea to do this book and to publish it. Second, I want to thank Anna Wunderlich, an amazing student at Hillsdale College interning at CURE this summer who perused through the 500 editorials I'd written to help select and summarize the few that would make this book. I also want to thank Bob Borens, my CURE colleague and researcher, who is my dearest friend and my collaborator in the writing of these columns. Thank you to my Pastor Doug Kessler and his wife Karen who let me rant on endlessly about every societal question and/or marginal idea. Thank you to my personal assistant Megan Conlon and the others on my CURE team who give me energy through their beautiful hearts. And, of course, a big thanks to our wonderful CURE donors who greatly encourage me as I act as a foot soldier in the public arena of fighting for freedom.

~ ~ ~

PART ONE: The Politics of Race

"We do need to remind ourselves that so many of the disparities that exist in the African-American community today can be directly traced to inequalities passed on from an earlier generation that suffered under the brutal legacy of slavery and Jim Crow."

Barack Obama

Slavery was abolished in our country nearly 150 years ago. But some blacks seem to think that they're still in chains. Accusations of racism abound in our society today, claims that blacks can't get ahead because whites keep pushing them down. This is the politics of race.

Numerous examples of success, from Cosby to Carson, defy this narrative created by liberal politicians, where conservatives are selfish bigots who despise and take advantage of the black community. Interestingly, these individuals have been rejected by the blindly conceited black leadership as traitors. Traitors to what? Traitors to divisive race politics, which only serve to isolate the very minorities they claim to help?

Those in the self-serving black leadership, more concerned with consolidating their political power than helping their own communities, have allowed their people to fall into moral pandemonium. These politicians, who use their race as an excuse for their own ineptitude, encourage their communities to do the same. As a result of their irresponsible behavior, the same problems that plague our nation plague the black community to an even greater degree. The loss of morality in our society has led to increased promiscuity and immoral behavior, causing chaos in black society.

The dark history of blacks in our country cannot be denied. But the future is bright. When blacks realize that the only chains holding them are the chains they place on themselves, they will take control of their future.

Race isn't going away, because the Democrats find it useful
May 3, 2014

Suddenly, we can't seem to get race out of the news.

9

Rep. Paul Ryan's tour around America's cities, trying to get a handle on America's persistent problems with poverty, turns into a racial incident as a member of the Congressional Black Caucus calls remarks he made in a radio interview "a thinly veiled racial attack (that) cannot be tolerated."

A simpleton lawbreaking rancher in Nevada, egged on by reporters, says stupid things about black Americans, and suddenly, he becomes a national figure with serious views about race.

And then a sleazy billionaire octogenarian -- a basketball team owner with a long history of racially charged remarks, some of which have resulted in lawsuits -- becomes front-page news when his equally sleazy young black Latina mistress records a private spat between them in which he makes tasteless comments about blacks.

Isn't race supposed to be behind us? Hasn't America elected, twice, a black man as its president?

But these days, our president is far less popular than he was when, with much fanfare, he was first elected.

Americans are not thrilled with his signature health care law, which has expanded the reach of government in an unprecedented way into the private lives of Americans and American businesses.

Economic news out this week shows that the American economy in the first quarter this year hardly grew at all, providing, according to The Wall Street Journal, "fresh evidence that the economic expansion that began almost five years ago remains the weakest in modern history."

Race is not going to go away, because it is too useful to the party of the left. In fact, it has never been so important.

Democrats are well aware of the profound demographic shifts in the nation today.

America is becoming decidedly less white, and the minority vote has and will continue to have increasing impact on the nation's future.

The Washington Post political blog The Fix ran a piece this week saying, "Black voters could decide who controls the Senate in 2015."

According to the piece, "six of the 16 states with the highest black populations are holding key Senate contests in 2014." And, it continues, three of these states -- Louisiana, North Carolina and Arkansas -- "are widely considered the most pivotal when it comes to the GOP's hopes of winning the majority."

High black turnout in these key states could extinguish Republican hopes of winning back the Senate.

A 2013 survey by the Pew Research Center reported that 46 percent of blacks feel there is "a lot" of racial discrimination today, compared with 16 percent of whites who do.

Democrats and the left-wing press know that fanning these still-racially sensitive flames is the way to turn out black voters.

Rep. Paul Ryan visited the Congressional Black Caucus this week to try to take the edge off the allegations thrown his way and talk about race and poverty. But why would 42 big-government-loving liberal black Democrats care about building bridges with a white Republican?

The Congressional Black Caucus isn't about ideas or solving problems. It is about political power. Black poverty hasn't changed since 1971, when the caucus was formed. But some present and former caucus members have become wealthy.

Conservatives waste time answering the race baiters. It's time to talk directly to minorities around the country about policies that would actually help these communities.

Ideas such as real, unconditional housing vouchers that would break the Department of Housing and Urban Development-induced ghettos and allow low-income Americans to live wherever they want.

Letting low-income earners opt out of payroll taxes and invest those funds in a private retirement account.

School choice programs permitting real education freedom and liberating black kids from teachers unions and failing public schools. And getting rid of minimum wage laws, which do nothing but increase unemployment among minority youth.

How to keep the poor poor
April 30, 2012

Media personality Tavis Smiley and Princeton philosophy professor Cornel West have just published their latest contribution to American poverty propaganda, "The Rich and the Rest of Us: A Poverty Manifesto."

The book should have a second subtitle: "How to keep the poor poor and blacks enslaved to government." To the extent this book is taken seriously by anyone, the result can only be more entrenched poverty.

Smiley and West's message is simple. America today consists of a few powerful, rapacious rich people and a lot of unfortunate, exploited poor people. The rich are rich because they are lucky. The poor are poor because they are unlucky. And the only way to solve the problem is activist government to manage the American economy and redistribute wealth.

It's as if the wealthy belonged to a different species of life with no common thread of humanity linking who they are to those who have less. The idea that "haves" once may have been "have-nots" -- or that that they did something to become "haves" that today's "have-nots" might consider doing -- never enters the equation.

Even if Smiley and West conceded that there may be some element of personal responsibility in how one's life turns out, their portrait is of an America now so unfair that personal responsibility is irrelevant. There is no hope for anyone to rise, according to this book, without government's boosting them using other people's money.

A good candidate for one of the more outrageous distortions, in a book filled with them, is No. 1 on their list of "Lies about poverty that America can no longer afford."

That No. 1 lie is: "Poverty is a character flaw." No way, according to the authors, is there a chance that poverty has anything to do with one's behavior. Rather, "the 150 million Americans in or near poverty are there as a result of unemployment, war, the Great Recession, corporate greed, and income inequality."

Given this insight -- that there are 150 million poor Americans whose economic condition is the result of extenuating circumstances -- it is no wonder that Smiley and West never once mention what many scholars see as the major causes of poverty -- poor education and family breakdown.

According to the Bureau of Labor Statistics, in 2011 unemployment for those without a high-school diploma was 50 percent higher than those with a high-school diploma and almost three times higher than it was for those with a college degree.

According to the Census Bureau, 17.8 percent of American families with children younger than 18 lived in poverty in 2010. However, in households with children who had married parents, 8.4 percent lived in poverty. In households with children headed by a single mother, 39.6 percent lived in poverty.

The evidence is powerful that getting educated and getting married dramatically reduce the prospects for living in poverty. Yet it's apparently not sufficiently powerful to interest Smiley and West in noting these factors once in their "poverty manifesto."

Can better government policy expand opportunity for those who actually choose to get educated and live responsible lives? Certainly. But what we need is totally the opposite of what these authors advocate. Evidence abounds that countries with limited government and more economic freedom are far and away the most prosperous.

Despite this book's message of the inherent hopelessness and unfairness of today's America, the authors themselves seem to be doing quite well, selling their paperback "poverty manifesto" at $12 a pop. Apparently, it's quite good business to tell Americans that America is unfair.

Perhaps this book can be used to reduce competition for jobs by immigrants.

According to the State Department, there are currently 4.6 million visa applicants wishing to enter the United States under the family and employment preferences immigration program. They apparently haven't gotten the word that America is no longer a land of opportunity.

The Race Factor

It's not about race; it's about how liberalism doesn't solve poverty
March 29, 2014

When Rep. Barbara Lee, D-Calif., went off on Rep. Paul Ryan, R-Wis., for his remarks that "we have got this tailspin of culture, in our inner cities in particular, of men not working and just generations of men not even thinking about working or learning the value and the culture of work," the wrong part of what she had to say got all the attention.

The big buzz that Congressional Black Caucus member Lee generated stemmed from her accusation that Ryan's remarks were a "thinly veiled racial attack."

But the part of her remarks I found most interesting was: "Mr. Ryan should step up and produce some legitimate proposals on how to tackle poverty and racial discrimination in America."

13

Ryan has been one of the most creative and courageous policy-thinkers in Washington in recent years.

Ryan sat down with me for an interview shortly before he ran for vice president in 2012. His thoughtfulness and compassion came through loud and clear, and he zeroed in on the core of a problem I have been talking and writing about for more than 20 years -- government programs that not only do not solve problems but make problems worse.

I stepped into this whole business of public policy from my own experience with welfare. I saw that the original welfare program -- which operated in this country from the 1960s until it was reformed in 1996 and required women to not work, not save and not get married in order to qualify for their welfare checks -- was an efficient mechanism to destroy family and perpetuate poverty.

So it should come as no surprise that single-parent black households tripled as a percentage of all black households from the 1960s to today.

Where Lee is right is that this is not about race. It's about liberalism.

The racial aspect comes into play in that black political leaders, such as Lee, overwhelmingly embrace liberalism, progressivism, welfare statism -- whatever you want to call it -- which has failed and caused an untold amount of damage in the very communities they claim to want to help. And they refuse to ever learn. Their answer to every problem, despite prior experience, is more government, more taxpayer dollars.

When real reformers, such as Ryan, come along, they get branded racist.

In a column I wrote a couple of years ago, I pointed out that the 41-member Congressional Black Caucus was uniformly composed of Democrats and had a 100 percent re-election rate. Also, the average poverty rate in their districts was 20.3 percent, and the average child poverty rate was 28.8 percent, both well above national averages.

Economist Walter Williams has pointed out that in America's 10 poorest cities with populations more than 250,000, "for decades, all of them have been run by Democratic and presumably liberal administrations. Some of them -- such as Detroit (now the largest municipal bankruptcy in the nation's history), Buffalo, Newark and Philadelphia -- haven't elected a Republican mayor for more than a half-century. What's more is that, in some cases for decades, the mayors of six of these high-poverty cities have been black Americans."

Again, the point is not that the mayors of these cities are black. It is that they are liberals. And black politicians, such as Lee, overwhelmingly are liberals, and they remain liberals despite a long and consistent track record of liberal policies' failure.

When welfare was reformed, liberals like Lee fought it.

It is pure self-absorption for people in any interest group to think it is all about them. America is in real trouble today, and we're all in this together.

Lee talks about "code words." Her code word is "racist," which means someone like Ryan, who wants to make Americans of all backgrounds better off by giving them more freedom, more choice, more responsibility and less government.

Pulling black America out of oblivion
July 17, 2006

So far this month, there have been 14 homicides in Washington. Almost one a day. Nearly 100 people have been murdered so far this year in the nation's capital. Robberies are up 18 percent, and assaults with a deadly weapon are up 14 percent.

District of Columbia police Chief Charles H. Ramsey has declared a "crime emergency."

This is the same Ramsey who, talking about homicides in the capital region several years ago, said: "The African-American community has to be central in the solution because that is where the problem lies and that is the community being hurt the most by this genocide. ... You've got generations of dysfunction, and that cycle has got to be broken."

It was Ramsey's words that, in part, inspired Bill Cosby to begin his campaign to deliver a message of personal responsibility into black communities and to black families.

Although Cosby's visits to inner cities around the country have been received with considerable local enthusiasm, his campaign has been far less well-received among the mainstream black political and intellectual leadership. That is to say, black liberals.

For these folks, Cosby has committed two great sins. One, a famous black man with a national audience of whites, as well as blacks, has stated that there are problems in the black community. Two, he has suggested that blacks need to look at themselves rather than at others to solve their problems.

According to Washington Post columnist Courtland Milloy, juvenile robberies in D.C. are up 95 percent this year, and he quotes Ramsey: "Young black males, in groups of five to six, ages 13 to 15, are displaying handguns and beating their victims." But perhaps more disturbing -- and revealing -- is Ramsey's observation that "we're dealing with adolescents who have no remorse, no regrets."

In response to a column I wrote recently about the Rev. Al Sharpton's chastising black churches for focusing too much on personal morality, I received a letter from a gentleman who identified himself as a "white minister." Here's part of it:

"My son was murdered by two teenage African-American boys. ... At the trial of the boy who pulled the trigger twice to kill my son, I looked into the boy's eyes. There was no remorse at all and he seemed like he didn't realize that life, anyone's life, had any value. This 19-year-old boy was a dropout of school. He had no family at the trial. It was like no one had given this boy any love."

The most recent murder in D.C. produced shock waves because of the location of the crime and the gratuitous violence involved. Three black youths, two in their 20s and one 15-year-old, allegedly attacked a young couple standing outside a mansion in the affluent Georgetown area at 2 a.m. last Sunday. The couple had just returned from a movie.

As one of the youths attempted to rape the woman, according to authorities, another slit the throat of her date, a young man visiting from Great Britain who was in Washington for an internship.

A police commander called the crime "one of the most brutal acts" he'd seen in his 19 years of police work.

The police have apprehended the suspects, and records indicate the suspected murderer told his accomplices before the assault that he was going to "cut" somebody.

Homicide is the No. 1 killer of black men. According to the Bureau of Justice Statistics, blacks are six times likelier to be the victim of homicide than whites, and blacks are seven times likelier to commit homicide than whites.

It should be clear that the problem is that America's black community is now suspended in a moral vacuum. Life is cheap and meaningless, and murder, sex, abortion and robbery are viewed with the same gravity as ordering a Big Mac and fries. There is no accountability, only blame. And this mindset continues to be nourished in both the street language of Sharpton and the Rev. Jesse Jackson and the fancy Harvard prose of Sen. Barack Obama.

In a recent speech of several thousand words about politics and religion, the Illinois Democrat never once mentioned personal responsibility but did manage to talk about the importance of diversity programs and condom distribution.

There is only one hope for pulling black America out of oblivion: re-instilling a sense of absolutes, of right and wrong, and doing this from the grass roots up, one person at a time. Anyone who thinks there is an alternative is kidding himself.

Blacks can continue to listen to the Sharptons, the Obamas and the black intellectuals who have a thousand different ways to say "it's not my fault." The price will be a black community lost forever.

Are racial designations real or just political?
Aug. 29, 2005

"Texas Becomes Newest 'Majority-Minority' State, Census Bureau Announces."

That was the headline of a recent U.S. Census Bureau press release noting that Texas has now joined Hawaii, New Mexico and California as a state whose "minority" population exceeds 50 percent of the state's population.

Who are minorities? According to the Census Bureau, "all people except non-Hispanic single-race whites."

It's no wonder that I've gotten a spate of calls from reporters trying to help them determine whether this Census Bureau announcement is as absurd as it sounds.

17

The press release continues in equally lucid fashion, introducing population statistics for all "minority" groups with this sentence: "The following race data are for people reporting their specified race, whether or not they reported any other races, and for Hispanics (who may be of any race)." If the source of this were not the United States government, I would assume there had to be some hidden logic not readily accessible to the casual lay reader.

But of course, there is no logic. This is about politics.

The list of "race" data, for which Hispanics are the reported exception, includes Asians. Are Asians a race? People from Japan and people from India look very different to me.

Regarding the idea of "race," according to historian Jacques Barzun, "no agreement seems to exist. ... Race seems to embody a fact as simple and as obvious as the noonday sun, but if that is so, why the endless wrangling about the idea and the facts of race. ... What is a race? How can it be recognized? Who constitute the several races?"

A clear definition of race itself eludes social scientists but does not seem to trouble Census Bureau bureaucrats.

Returning to the press release, we are informed at its conclusion that "the federal government treats Hispanic origin and race as distinct concepts."

What exactly is "Hispanic origin"?

According to historian Paul Johnson, the historic origin of Hispanic is not ethnicity but politics: "The Mexican-American Legal Defense and Education Fund, a powerful interest-group in alliance with the Democratic Party, succeeded in establishing a racial category known as 'Hispanic,' which included Latin mestizos; people of predominantly European, black, and American Indian descent; descendants of long-assimilated Californios and Tejanos; and other groups who once spoke Spanish -- almost anyone, in fact who found it advantageous to belong, so long as they could not be accused of being 'Caucasian' or 'Aryan.' This pseudo race came into existence as the result of statistical classification by bureaucrats."

Johnson goes on and relates other shenanigans that resulted in establishing the various so-called racial categories used by the Census Bureau -- American Indian, Alaska Native, Asian, Pacific Islander, black and white -- and determinants of which ethnicities belong in which group.

Is this what America is about? How did we get to this?

It created somewhat of a stir in the black community when the Census Bureau reported several years ago that Hispanics had surpassed blacks as the nation's largest "minority" group.

The only reason anyone would care about this is that the very odious attitudes and ideas that historically provided the rationale for discrimination and persecution have been transformed into platforms for political power, preferences and entitlements.

It is ironic to me that as we encourage Iraqis to create a new, free society in the Middle East -- as Sunni Muslims, Shiite Muslims and Kurds work to create a constitution with just and common rules for governing all -- we Americans retain the concepts of race and ethnicity in our political formalities. I think it is insulting to all Americans and denigrates the ideal of freedom as we understand it at home and advocate it abroad.

My plea here, of course, is not to ignore ethnic differences. They are crucial. My plea is to remove them from politics, where, rather than being appreciated as part of individual uniqueness, they are used to transform people into objects for political manipulation.

Back to Jacques Barzun: "The race question appears a much bigger affair than a trumped-up excuse for local persecution. ... It defaces every type of mental activity -- history, art, politics, science and social reform."

If the idea of race is elusive and abusive, the notion of minority is, of course, absurd. Hence we get ridiculous headlines like the Census Bureau's about a "majority-minority."

A truly free society understands and respects the fact that there really is just one minority -- each unique individual. Certainly, this was the Rev. Martin Luther King's point about "content of character" being the standard to which we should aspire.

Sellouts or Truth Tellers

Ben Carson endures predictable liberal assault
April 15, 2013

Dr. Ben Carson stepped into the national spotlight in February, when, speaking at the National Prayer Breakfast to an audience that included President Barack Obama, he openly criticized the president's approach to health care and his overall management of the nation's economy.

19

Carson, who is director of pediatric neurosurgery at Johns Hopkins Hospital, is a hero to many. His rise from a Detroit ghetto to a life of accomplishment and distinction is a story of American ideals on steroids.

Those ideals say that America is about merit, not circumstance. Your life, your achievements are the result of what you do and how you live, not where you came from.

The hard history of blacks in America has always made it a challenge for them to accept this credo. Many still carry a sense that those ideals may be true for whites but never have been true for blacks.

So in this context, Carson's story is particularly important. It's making liberals nervous, and the attacks on him are starting.

He's now pulled out, under pressure, from giving the commencement address at Johns Hopkins University because some are unhappy with how, in an interview on Fox News Channel, he expressed his views regarding the importance of maintaining the integrity of traditional marriage.

Blacks have known about Carson for years. I gave his book "Gifted Hands" to my daughters to read when they were little girls. A highly acclaimed made-for-TV movie about his life aired in 2009, with Carson played by Oscar-winning actor Cuba Gooding Jr.

But this story of personal responsibility, hard work and traditional values is becoming a political story. It is becoming political because Ben Carson's American dream story, according to the liberal script, is not supposed to work for blacks.

Carson is the biggest threat to liberals since Bill Cosby got out of line at an NAACP banquet in 2004 in Washington, D.C.

Cosby had the temerity to deliver tough, critical talk about what too many blacks are doing with the freedom that civil rights activists of the 1960s fought to achieve.

He contrasted the '60s generation with the new generation of black youths sitting in jail: "These are not political criminals. These are people going around stealing Coca-Cola. People getting shot in the back of the head over a piece of poundcake."

Cosby attributed the chaos to a breakdown in values, family and personal responsibility. It's the last thing the NAACP crowd wanted to hear that night, and Cosby paid a price. He was vilified and marginalized until he backed off.

Liberals never take on what black conservatives actually say, because they can't. So the attacks become personal.

Trillions of tax dollars have been poured into black communities over the past half-century, producing virtually no change in the incidence of black poverty.

Yet Carson, through diligence and traditional values, achieved on his own what those trillions of dollars of government programs were supposed to deliver.

Liberal black writer Ta-Nehisi Coates put the cards on the table in an article about Cosby that appeared in The Atlantic in 2008. The typical black conservative votes for Democrats, he noted, "not out of love for abortion rights ... but because he feels ... that the modern-day GOP draws on support of people who hate him."

Stoking paranoia about racism has always been the strategy of liberals to fend off the political threat of conservative values that so many church-going blacks embrace.

Predictably, Coates has produced a New York Times column on Carson, reducing this great man to the usual caricature of a black empty suit manipulated by white conservatives.

Ben Carson is an accomplished and wealthy man. Americans, certainly black Americans, need him in public life more than he needs to be in public life. Let's hope the left wing and the haters of traditional morality don't succeed in making him conclude it's not worth it.

Why liberals hate Thomas, Palin
March 28, 2011

In days when slavery was legal in this country, all slaves did not willingly resign to the grim fate cast upon them.

The human spirit longs to be free. In some individuals, that longing beats so strongly in their breast that they will take large personal risks, against great odds, to rebel against tyranny that has transformed their life into a tool for someone else's will and whim.

Slaves who had the temerity to run away from their plantation "home" paid dearly if they were caught and returned. Measures were taken to make them an example to others who might harbor similar thoughts about freedom.

Among those measures were brutal public beatings of rebels, to which other slaves were forced to bear witness, digesting with great clarity the price of rebelliousness.

Such is the fate today of those uppity souls who choose to challenge the authority and legitimacy of our inexorably growing government plantation.

Those with interests for the care and feeding of this plantation cannot physically punish these rebels with the whip.

Their whip is the mainstream media, and the means of punishment of this virtual whip is not beating of a physical body but assassination of character.

This perspective helps us understand the ongoing liberal obsession with destroying Supreme Court Justice Clarence Thomas and former Alaska Gov. Sarah Palin.

Thomas and Palin are particularly threatening to liberals because their lives fly in the face of liberal mythology. According to this mythology, the essential and ongoing struggle in our nation is a power struggle of interests between "haves" and "have-nots" rather than an ongoing struggle for human freedom.

According to this mythology, there is an elite class of "haves," who, by virtue of fate and birth, control power and wealth. They are conservative because their only interest is to keep things as they are.

Fighting against this conservative elite are noble "have-nots," struggling, by any means possible, to get their fair share and against wealth distributed by an unjust and blind fate.

A high-profile conservative whose very life and personal history poses an open challenge and affront to this mythology is a liberal's worst nightmare.

If being a conservative means simply protecting the bounty passed on to you by your forebears, why would a man from a poor black family in the South or a woman from a white working-class family in Alaska be a conservative -- no less a conservative whose conservatism plays a role in a successful professional life?

The liberal answer is that the only way this could be possible is that this is an individual of dubious character, on the take and being paid off handsomely by conservative powers that be.

After all, in the liberal mindset, the government plantation, carefully grown and nurtured by liberals over these years, supposedly on behalf of our unfortunate "have-nots," should be the natural home for anyone of modest background and no inheritance.

Not only should that individual want to live on the plantation but you'd think he or she would want to participate in the noble cause of keeping it growing.

The federal government plantation now sucks out one-quarter of our economy. Seventy percent of federal spending now amounts to checks government cuts and mails to individuals.

Where does it all lead? Look at Detroit. This is a government plantation poster child and a portent of our nation's future if this keeps up.

The human spirit does long to be free. Many understand this but are intimidated to speak up. Some are brave and do speak up.

Those who are successful and who know there is no future on the plantation will be publicly flogged by the overseers. Such is the case of Justice Thomas and Mrs. Palin.

But it is brave individuals such as this, in public and private life, upon whom our future depends.

Bill Cosby's words enrage but also enlighten
June 8, 2004

Bill Cosby conducted his own shock-and-awe campaign recently at festivities celebrating the 50th anniversary of the Brown v. Board of Education school desegregation decision.

He used his remarks to an audience of a virtual who's who in the black political establishment to redirect attention from political and legal victories of the past to the dismal social reality of the present. Cosby crossed the line by laying out the tragic state of affairs of inner-city black life today and then accused blacks themselves of being responsible for the mess.

One can only imagine the gasps throughout an audience for whom being black is not just a condition but also a profession. These are folks who have built careers finding explanations for every black social malady except the irresponsible behavior of individuals themselves.

The premise that being born black and poor in America is a dead end has defined black politics for the past half-century. Black political careers have been built on peddling the message that the American dream is a white dream and that the only way blacks have a prayer of making it in America is through government intervention.

However, more than his words, Bill Cosby's life challenges this premise. In the midst of the turmoil of the 1960s, Cosby, born black and poor, was making it in America.

As a stand-up comedian in the early '60s, he was making all Americans laugh with his insight and cleverness -- and not with cheap vulgarity. In 1963, a year before the Civil Rights Act was passed, he was standing in as host for Johnny Carson on America's most popular late-night talk and variety show. By 1965, when the political class dreamed up affirmative action as the necessary formula for black success, Cosby became the first black man to star in a predominantly white television drama series, "I Spy."

I have often made the point that the civil rights movement after Dr. Martin Luther King Jr. amounted to a politicization of Dr. King's moral crusade. What happened is ironic. What, after all, is racism but the treatment of human beings as objects? Dr. King's plea that character, not race, be the guiding principle of human relationships was an appeal to elevate humanity and appreciate the uniqueness of every individual.

Unfortunately, the defining ideas of post-King black politics had more in common with racism than the humanism of King. The politics of categories and quotas returned human beings to the realm of objects.

Values and responsibility were taken off the table, and victimization and blame became the themes. It is no wonder that during the past 40 years, the inner-city black family has all but disintegrated and inner-city communities have become defined by crime, drugs, disease, promiscuity and abortion.

Truth ultimately always has its way, and more and more blacks, particularly young blacks, are seeing it. They want to recapture their humanity and want to be liberated from the prison of racial politics. Polls show movement of young blacks away from the political establishment, with more and more defining themselves as politically independent. Consider Al Sharpton's disastrous presidential bid. Being black just isn't a political platform anymore.

Sharp eyes in the leadership of both political parties should see the opportunities here. A tight presidential race is upon us, and swing votes in a handful of states can make all the difference. For increasing numbers of blacks, business-as-usual party politics simply amounts to a battle between which party's status quo will be preserved. Neither is of much interest to those already disenfranchised.

Political candidates of both parties should listen to the truth of the street, made clear and public by Bill Cosby. Today's challenge in black America is the restoration of humanity and the recapturing of personal responsibility. Platforms that capture this theme will capture the hearts and minds of those in the inner city, who can help decide who occupies the White House next year.

Let's talk about schools that respond to the discipline and creative forces of the marketplace. Remove the heavy hand of government from education and allow parental choice and citizens of all colors will respond.

Let's start telling the truth about a bankrupt Social Security system that systematically prevents low-income workers from saving and accumulating wealth. Allow Americans of all colors to opt out and use these funds to open their own personal retirement accounts. Let's fix a bureaucratized health care system that minimizes individual control over their funds and choices.

And let's keep faith, family and values, not politics and government, at center stage.

Thank you, Bill Cosby, for telling the truth. America is listening.

The Great Divide

Why do blacks still buy the government plantation lie?
Nov. 15, 2010

Almost two years ago, a new Democratic administration and Congress took control of Washington. They immediately sent out invitations to the American people.

"You are cordially invited onto the government plantation. P.S. We're in charge, but you pick up the tab. RSVP by Nov. 2, 2010."

The RSVPs have poured in, and the majority of Americans have replied: "Sorry. We've got other plans."

But it was mostly white voters who turned down this invitation.

Why are blacks, who know life on the government plantation better than whites and who are proportionately being hit much harder in this difficult economy, still buying what working-class whites have rejected hands down -- that, as Karl Rove put it, "we can spend our way to prosperity"?

25

The problem is broader and deeper. Blacks, by and large, still see government dependence as the remedy rather than the disease, despite overwhelming evidence to the contrary. They still choose to listen to left-wing black political leadership and media who have careers in keeping it all going.

Consider that it was welfare-state government policies that caused this economic collapse to begin with and that it was community activist groups claiming to represent the interests of minorities who lobbied for these policies.

According to a new study by American Enterprise Institute scholar Edward Pinto, a former executive vice president and chief credit officer at Fannie Mae, this is exactly what happened.

The recession was caused, according to Pinto, by the collapse of housing and mortgage markets. Markets imploded because of the proliferation of risky unconventional mortgages, which spread as a result of government dictates to promote "affordable housing."

It was community activist groups such as National People's Action and ACORN -- yes, the old stomping buddies of our president's -- that lobbied for taxpayer-backed lending behemoths Fannie Mae and Freddie Mac to relax lending standards.

The result was a new law passed in 1992 directing new "affordable housing mandates" on Freddie and Fannie.

After this, as Pinto tells the story, the Department of Housing and Urban Development issued new liberalized lending guidelines, directing that "lending institutions, secondary market investors (and) mortgage insurers ... should work collaboratively to reduce homebuyer down payment requirements."

A widespread change in the mortgage lending landscape followed.

Whereas in 1990, a tiny fraction of mortgages had down payments less than 3 percent, by 2006, "an estimated 30 percent of all homebuyers put no money down."

According to Pinto's AEI colleague Peter Wallison, by 2008, almost 50 percent of loans were subprime, and two-thirds of them were held by government agencies or firms required to buy them by government regulations.

In the short run, these government directives relaxing lending standards to promote homeownership were wildly successful. Homeownership rates climbed to record levels.

Of course, HUD, Fannie and Freddie could push all this because the assumption lurking behind it all was that if it collapsed, U.S. taxpayers were there to pick up the tab.

Hey, government bureaucrats actually got something right.

Now we are left cleaning up the mess and picking up the pieces. But a tragic and ironic footnote is that black Americans, whose interests community activist groups who lobbied for all this were supposedly representing, have taken the brunt.

Blacks, whose homeownership rates skyrocketed during the government-stoked boom, now have foreclosure rates twice that of whites. And of course, black unemployment in this economic slowdown following the collapse is double that of whites.

If there was a moment of doubt that most Americans were going to buy into the government plantation lie, the most recent elections should clear things up.

But the midterm elections also tell us we still have a divided country, and many who bought the big government lie in the past still aren't getting it.

We've got a lot of work to do.

Today's NAACP symptom of black problems
March 12, 2007

Bruce Gordon, who has resigned as president of the NAACP, got a crash course in the difference between the world of politics and the world of business. The former is driven by power and control, the latter by markets and service.

It's why countries with more of the former and less of the latter tend to be poorer than those where it is the other way around.

And it is ironic that the NAACP, an organization born with an agenda to advance freedom, over time has morphed into an organization defined in every dimension by the culture of politics.

Gordon, a businessman and corporate executive by career, made a bad business call. He assessed the situation he was getting into incorrectly and learned, as we say, the hard way. He thought they wanted him to solve problems and build a better organization. They -- or, maybe more precisely, Julian Bond, the NAACP's chairman -- were looking for someone to carry their political baggage.

Meanwhile, it's obvious that an organization whose president quits 19 months after he was hired to replace a predecessor who himself left under duress is a troubled organization. If the NAACP were publicly traded, its stock would be sinking.

It's clear that the organization that Bruce Gordon decided to go to work for was not the organization he thought it was.

One reason may be that the NAACP today is not the organization it once was.

Founded in 1909, the NAACP had clear challenges in the beginning. The legal and institutional barriers to equal treatment and due process under the law for blacks were real and tangible. It required no subtlety of thought to understand what the battle was that needed to be fought, although there were differences of opinion regarding how best to fight the battle.

With the passage of the Civil Rights Act and the Voting Rights Act in 1964 and 1965, that battle was won. That's not to say the struggle was over. Life's struggles are never over. But it became a different battle.

Once the chains are broken, the challenge translates into a human struggle of realizing one's potential in freedom. The battlefield moves from outside to inside.

But the black political leadership didn't want to let go. It wanted to keep the game political.

Today the NAACP has simply become a rote platform for left-wing politics.

For reasons that I'll leave to others to explain, the organization has become more highly motivated to promote this left-wing agenda than to address the many problems of its own community.

Discussing his departure in an interview with Tavis Smiley, Gordon observed, "In business terminology, we would argue that organizations that are no longer customer-focused, who lose the heart of the customer, who lose the choice of the customer, will ultimately fail."

Practically speaking, Gordon's observations are borne out by the following:

Barely 1 in 4 blacks support legalization of gay marriage. Yet one would be hard-pressed to find a lawsuit pushing for gay marriage in which the NAACP is not a plaintiff.

Black support for school vouchers is stronger than white support. Almost 3 in 4 blacks between the ages of 26 and 35 support vouchers.

Yet the NAACP adamantly opposes vouchers and school choice. A great victory was just achieved in the state of Utah, which will open the door to vouchers. NAACP opposition to Utah's new law is posted prominently on the home page of its website.

It's a similar story with personal Social Security accounts. Young blacks poll strongly in favor. The NAACP opposes.

Even moderate black journalists now recognize and write that the challenge in black America today is social. AIDS, abortion, family breakdown, crime, poor education -- these are problems of values and lifestyle, not politics.

Yet like the old saw that to a man with a hammer everything looks like a nail, NAACP leaders interpret the clear moral and social crisis in our inner cities as a political problem in need of government solutions. Ironically, and tragically, it was the invasion of government into family life, through the welfare state, that precipitated black family breakdown to begin with.

To Bruce Gordon's credit, he wanted to transform the NAACP into an organization in which blacks take responsibility for identifying and trying to solve the problems in their own community.

This was obviously too much for an organization that wants to pursue "social justice" in a world in which most black babies are born with no father at home.

The NAACP has become a symptom of the problems in black America rather than a source for solutions. Perhaps this latest crisis will provoke some badly needed soul-searching and change.

Racism again? Really?
July 26, 2010

Can anyone tell me why suddenly race is the hot topic of national discourse?

According to Gallup polling of last week, the issues most on the minds of Americans are the economy and jobs, followed by dissatisfaction with all aspects of government.

I didn't notice racism on the list anywhere.

The NAACP says it was "snookered" by Fox News on the Shirley Sherrod story.

I say we've all been snookered by the NAACP.

The NAACP has shown that those who have written this organization off as irrelevant are wrong. It demonstrated this past week that if it so chooses, it can dominate the national discussion with its racial agenda, regardless of what the real pressing issues of national concern may be.

The accusation about tea party racism is ridiculous. But even if you don't think it's ridiculous, is this the discussion we need to be having when national unemployment hovers at 10 percent and when black unemployment is closer to 15 percent, double that of whites?

Now, of course we should be talking about racism if this is what is driving black unemployment. But is it?

I don't think so. Nor do most blacks.

In January of this year, well into this economic downturn and well into the emergence of the tea party movement, the Pew Research Center surveyed black attitudes.

In answer to the question "When blacks don't make progress, who or what is to blame?" 52 percent of blacks responded that "blacks" themselves are "mostly responsible," and 34 percent said "racism." This is the reverse of how blacks responded to this question just 15 years ago, when 56 percent said that racism was the impediment to black progress.

In the same survey, blacks responded almost identically as whites to the question of whether success in life is "determined by forces beyond one's control" or whether "everyone has the power to succeed."

Seventy-seven percent of blacks and 82 percent of whites said that "everyone has the power to succeed," and 16 percent of blacks and 12 percent of whites said success is "determined by forces beyond one's control."

And when blacks were asked in this same survey about the main problems facing black families, the response was overwhelmingly the same as the general result of the Gallup poll of last week. Jobs.

So Americans of all colors today generally feel responsible for their own lives, and the main concern of most is the sick state of our economy.

So let's have that discussion.

Clearly, there are differences of opinion about how to light a fire under this economy and the role of government. Some think government is the answer. Some think it's the problem.

But this is a difference of opinion about how the world works. Why are we talking about racism?

Racism is about people being persecuted and endangered because of their color. It's about not being treated equally under the law or being denied access to public facilities or work because of one's color.

Fortunately, those ugly days are behind us. And aside from the political and legal truths that verify this, black attitudes themselves, as the Pew data bear out, support it. And if we need further verification, sitting in the White House is a black man who is there with the help of 43 percent of the votes of white Americans.

Talk about racism may help employment for those in the race business. But it has little relevance to getting the American economy working again, which is what we should be single-mindedly focused on.

And allowing race to become the focus of public discourse shuts out the very message that blacks need to hear: that they are disproportionately hurt by an economic downturn being prolonged by excessive government growth and interference.

~ ~ ~

PART TWO: Culture Wars

"I've got two daughters, 9 years old and 6 years old. I am going to teach them first of all about values and morals. But if they make a mistake, I don't want them punished with a baby."

Barack Obama

We are a nation at war. Families are torn apart by violence and lies. Thousands of children are murdered in our streets every day. The pillars of our society are being ripped to shreds. The enemy? Ourselves.

Our nation was founded on virtues and boundaries and ideals drawn directly from the Bible -- virtues such as traditional values and personal responsibility. These virtues and ideals are what hold our country together. But today the boundaries are being challenged throughout our society, and traditional virtues and ideals have become subjective. Fundamental concepts such as conjugal marriage, protection for human life, common decency and manners are being cast aside in favor of moral relativism and unabashed narcissism.

The blindly conceited in this battle embraces this moral relativism as a sort of quasi-religion where the individual becomes his own god and all else must fall to his will. He engages in battle against anything and everything that is opposed to his amoral lifestyle, including the family, religion, morality and even society itself.

"Of all the dispositions and habits which lead to political prosperity," George Washington warned, "religion and morality are indispensable supports." Without the religious values that come from our Judeo-Christian heritage, our nation is doomed to self-destruction. This is a battle we cannot let them win. We must fight back.

Defining the conservative-versus-liberal divide
April 26, 2010

Now that President Barack Obama is getting ready to make his second Supreme Court nomination, the usual banter is taking place about the court and judicial philosophy.

The Supreme Court, of course, profoundly influences the character of our country.

Although, for instance, many look back on the policies of Franklin Roosevelt and his New Deal programs as the beginning of the real growth of the American welfare state, it is really key Supreme Court decisions during that time that enabled all of this. Court decisions changing the interpretation of "general welfare," interstate commerce and the authority of the federal government to tax changed the game and opened a new era of big government.

At the beginning of the 1930s, the federal government's take of national gross domestic product was a little over 10 percent. By the mid-1940s, it was over 20 percent, and the trend has been only upward since.

Although much of the discussion about judicial philosophy contrasts how conservative and liberal judges relate to the Constitution, I think the real key to conservative and liberal divergence is the worldview these judges already have when they sit down to interpret the Constitution.

The statement of vision defining American values appears in the Declaration of Independence. Understanding that vision is where I think the most fundamental conservative-versus-liberal divide exists.

Consider how President Obama relates to the Constitution. He wrote in his book "The Audacity of Hope," "Implicit in its structure, in the very idea of ordered liberty, was a rejection of absolute truth."

Our president is a moral relativist. So we may expect that he doesn't take very seriously the idea, as stated in the Declaration of Independence, that there are absolutes -- that we have God-given rights that precede government and that the job of government is to secure them.

Rather than see government's job as securing our rights, the liberal sees it as inventing them. The politician -- or the sympathetic judge -- defines what is moral and just.

There's a lot of speculation about what is driving the tea party movement and why, but as reflected in the latest survey by the Pew Research Center, Americans' trust in government is at an all-time low.

I think that most fundamentally, its discomfort with this moral relativism is what is driving the pervasive unrest.

The whole unique idea of American government -- the idea of human liberty -- was that there are absolute truths and that individual citizens can and must be protected from arbitrary rulers, whether it is a king or a political class with arbitrary powers.

President Obama said the other day regarding the kind of court nominee he will seek, "I want somebody who is going to be interpreting our Constitution in a way that takes into account individual rights."

What in the world can this possibly mean from our president, who has just signed into law a health care bill that will force every single American citizen to buy a government-defined health insurance policy? It's a health care law that opens the door to unprecedented government control over how private individuals manage their health care and the most private decisions they make for their own lives.

What can it possibly mean coming from a president who opposed the Supreme Court's decision a few years ago banning partial-birth abortion -- which is purely and simply the torturing and murdering of a live infant?

The real differences between liberal and conservative judges are most fundamentally about the world in which Americans will live -- whether we live and will live in a nation in which there are absolute truths or we will live in one in which we are at the hands of political arbitrariness and our lives and property are up for grabs.

Our country is being governed today by those with the latter view of the world, but fortunately, more and more Americans are deeply concerned.

When color trumps Christianity
July 6, 2009

President Obama hosted a reception at the White House celebrating LGBT (lesbian, gay, bisexual and transgender) Pride Month. Black Christians should take note and learn a few things about our black president.

As they say, we are what we do.

It tells us something that Obama had no time to host an event for the National Day of Prayer.

Nor did he have time to accept the invitation to convey greetings and a few remarks to the few hundred thousand who came to Washington, as they do every January, for the March for Life.

However, the LGBT pride event did make it onto the president's busy schedule.

Here are parts of his remarks that I think are noteworthy for black Christians:

First, we now know that Obama buys into reasoning equating the homosexual political movement to the black civil rights movement: "It's not for me to tell you to be patient any more than it was for others to counsel patience to African-Americans who were petitioning for equal rights a half-century ago."

Perhaps Obama can extend some of his famous empathy to a black Christian woman, Crystal Dixon, who lost her University of Toledo job for writing a column in her local paper challenging this premise. Dixon was fired for being uppity enough to write: "I take great umbrage at the notion that those choosing the homosexual lifestyle are 'civil rights victims.' ... I cannot wake up tomorrow and not be a black woman."

Considering our president's priorities, I recall a song popular during the civil rights movement: "Which Side Are You On?"

Second, Obama sees the black community as being a little slow on the uptake to grasp that homosexuality and same-sex marriage are OK. There still are those, according to him, "who don't yet fully embrace their gay brothers and sisters." He deals with this, he said, by talking about it in front of "unlikely audiences," such as "in front of African-American church members."

Maybe a lot of us black folks still readin' our Bibles just haven't had enough of that Harvard learnin'.

And third, Obama talked about HIV/AIDS but didn't bother to mention that it's overwhelmingly blacks whom this scourge is killing.

Why would our black president discuss HIV/AIDS and not mention that although blacks represent 12 percent of our population, they account for 50 percent of HIV/AIDS cases and half of HIV-related deaths? Or that the incidence of HIV/AIDS infection per every 100,000 people is nine times higher among blacks than whites?

Of course, it would have been bad form for Obama to sour the punch bowl at the LBGT Pride Month festivities by mentioning the disproportionate toll this lifestyle takes on blacks.

Blacks, of course, made the difference in getting Proposition 8 passed in California, which defined marriage as between a man and a woman. They then switched over and voted for Obama.

Obama has said he opposes same-sex marriage. Can this really be so? He said at the White House event that he's called for Congress to repeal the Defense of Marriage Act. DOMA is the main obstacle to nationalizing legalization of same-sex marriage.

Black Christians have a lot of soul-searching to do. We know the pain of black history. But we also must retain clarity that these many injustices were the result of race and color's trumping Christian principles.

How can black Christians do this to themselves? How can black Christians allow race and color to trump Christian principles in driving their support for a leader -- particularly as sexually transmitted diseases kill our people, when a third of abortions are black babies and when the only hope for future black prosperity is restoration of the black family?

Eternal Truths

We have a national crisis in character
Nov. 19, 2012

Here's an excerpt from a letter I received the other day from a college professor:

"Throughout this election I discussed with students the differences between ideologies. The majority of them are on federal financial aid. They are fine with more taxes as long as they will be taken care of. It is disturbing to hear that they are willing to spend their own money on tattoos and cellphones but cannot buy the book for class until the financial aid comes in."

For those who see social conservatism as an annoyance and argue that Republicans must purge this agenda from their party to survive, I say: "Think again."

If Republicans want revival, we need an honest focus on what's really wrong in America and what must be done to ensure that a great nation will be standing for our grandchildren and great-grandchildren.

This kind of thinking is different from polls and focus groups and clever schemes to manage media and voter turnout.

Leadership is about identifying the truth, believing it and telling it in a way that people can grasp. Then they will respond and follow.

The professor's letter provides a snapshot, a hint, of what America's most basic problem is today. It's a problem of character and values.

Having lectured on more than 180 college campuses over the past 20 years, I have seen exactly what the professor is talking about.

Of course, government is too big. But how did it get this way? Americans vote every two years. They voted every two years during the whole period over which government grew to its current unwieldy size.

With the majority of the country now on one kind of government program or another, does anybody really think we can change this without talking about the human attitudes and values that produced it?

Democrats have a much easier problem than Republicans. They are not trying to change America. The trends and attitudes that got the whole country on welfare and produced the moral relativism that is destroying our families and character is the platform of the Democratic Party.

Democratic politicians have just one job: Deny the patient is sick.

The Republican Party, if it is going to be a real opposition party, has a much tougher job.

With all the talk about the recent election's being driven by demographics and turnout, the most basic point is the party and its candidate did not step up as a serious, principled opposition party.

We can't save Medicare and Social Security. They are bankrupt. Did we hear this from the Republican candidate? We heard wishy-washy words about reforming these systems so we can save them.

Did we hear anything about how our public schools -- controlled by unions whose agenda is growing their benefits and promoting moral relativism among our youth -- are destroying our children and our future? No.

When Ronald Reagan was first elected in November 1980, 18 percent of our babies were born to unwed mothers. Today 42 percent are. Anyone who thinks this is not a crisis of the first order can just as easily vote for a Democrat as a Republican.

Americans just re-elected a president who opposed the Supreme Court decision banning partial-birth abortion. The leader of our nation thinks it should be legal in America to kill a live, fully formed infant. What does this say about America today and our future?

There may be Republicans who think that we can ignore the crisis in character and values that underlie our fiscal crisis. There may be Republicans who think that if we have a better tax system, it doesn't matter if we have a country of single mothers, sexually ambiguous and confused men, and abortion and euthanasia on demand.

Ignoring these things would mean not just the end of the Republican Party but also the end of our country.

A society with no standards
July 20, 2004

Currently sitting at the top of the Billboard Hot 100 list is a song called "Confessions Part II," by R & B star Usher, in which Usher sings about having to tell his girlfriend he got another woman pregnant. There's a remix of the song featuring rapper Joe Budden. Here are Budden's words of wisdom:

"Pray that she abort that. And if she's talkin' 'bout keeping it, one hit to the stomach, she's leakin' it."

If she won't listen to reason and abort, punch her in the stomach.

Pro-life organizations, including Care Net, on whose board I sit, have protested this sickening, depraved and demented message. Island Def Jam, Usher's label, and LaFace/Zomba, Budden's label, of course, have declined comment. However, Budden himself was kind enough to comment and share his impeccable logic about the reasonableness of his approach on this matter.

"When you get somebody pregnant, you can make some suggestions, but the bottom line is (women) have the end say-so. ... As a guy, you wonder, 'What can I do to take that power away?' ... I might stir up a lot of confusion, but if you don't like it, turn it off."

Let's keep in mind that American kids, a good portion of whom are middle-class white kids, now shell out a few billion dollars a year to buy and listen to this garbage. So the artists have a point that hey, they're just serving up what the market wants.

Given the power of the marketplace and the protections of the First Amendment, it appears that there is not much to do here but, as Budden suggests, turn it off if you don't want to hear it.

Several years ago, rap impresario Russell Simmons, in response to growing outrage about rap music, organized a hip-hop summit in New York City. Rappers came, as did many black leaders, including Kweisi Mfume, Louis Farrakhan and members of the Congressional Black Caucus. When it was over, the president of the Hip-Hop Summit Action Network, Benjamin Chavis, summed it all up by saying, "We are taking back responsibility." Simmons himself followed up by saying, "Taking responsibility for the uplift of the poor and those who are underprivileged is more than just a noble goal. It makes good business sense."

So much for any illusions that rappers would be seized by a noble sense of social responsibility, put aside the prodigious financial rewards they get from peddling depravity and start rapping about love and marriage.

Is our only challenge now to just guess how deep the cesspool can get?

I've been writing a lot about Bill Cosby's recent provocative remarks challenging poor blacks to take personal responsibility. Cosby said, "For me, there is a time ... when we have to turn the mirror around."

Perhaps all Americans should listen to Cosby and think about turning the mirror around.

When rapper Joe Budden talks about his frustration with the power that the woman has to determine whether or not to abort, we should ask ourselves, "Who gave her this power over life and death?"

The answer in our secular society is the U.S. Supreme Court.

When the Supreme Court ruled in 1973 that abortion is a private matter, that there is no public standard relevant to the question of a woman's destroying her own fetus, it officially cut the umbilical cord, so to speak, that connected the private individual to any prevailing moral or social standards associated with the consequences of sexual behavior.

It removed any residual sense that as a society we see any sacred component to sexual behavior or its natural consequences.

There was a time when our sense of the sacred defined the framework through which we related to life and death. Now that the sacred has been banished from our public life, we leave these matters to the whim of any child from any broken home.

Today 7 in 10 black babies are born to unwed mothers. Those seven babies will, in all likelihood, grow up in an environment where -- whether they look at home, in their neighborhood, on the TV they watch, in the music they hear or to those who set the laws of our land -- the message they'll get is whatever they feel like doing is OK. If a young woman wants to sleep around, that's up to her. And if she wants to abort the result of her liaison, that's also her call.

No wonder Joe Budden is so frustrated. If it doesn't make any difference whether she gives in to his desires, if they are both equally not responsible, why shouldn't they both be equally not responsible or responsible for what to do with the pregnancy?

How can we call Joe Budden anti-social in a society with no social standards?

Obama has little in common with Lincoln
Jan. 19, 2009

It's ironic that Barack Obama chooses to infuse these opening days of his presidency with the imagery of Abraham Lincoln.

I don't think there could be two more different men. Understanding why may help us think about what to expect in the days ahead.

Beyond his trademark "change we can believe in," Obama's defining theme has been unity and inclusiveness. "There's not a liberal America and a conservative America; there's the United States of America. ... We worship an awesome God in the blue states ... and have gay friends in the red states."

Obama, of course, does not suggest that we don't have differences. His point is that those differences are not critically important and they're getting in our way. Let's put differences aside, get practical and solve our problems.

The inaugural ceremonies have pastors for everyone. A white evangelical who opposes same-sex marriage, a white homosexual, a left-wing black male and a left-wing black female.

His economic stimulus plan has large government expenditures to please Democrats and tax benefits to please Republicans.

Lincoln, too, sought unity. But Lincoln's notion of where national unity would lie was far different from Obama's.

He prophetically stated the challenge after accepting the Republican nomination for the Senate in 1858.

"A house divided against itself cannot stand. I believe this government cannot endure permanently half slave and half free. I do not expect the union to be dissolved -- I do not expect the house to fall -- but I do expect it will cease to be divided. It will become all one thing or all the other."

As historian Harry Jaffa points out, "for Lincoln, as for Jefferson and for all genuine supporters of the principles of the Declaration of Independence, the distinction between right and wrong is antecedent to any form of government and is independent of any man's or any majority's will."

Lincoln knew that some principles are so fundamental they cannot be compromised. He knew that we couldn't ignore our key differences. Unity could only come from facing them and making the hard choices.

He knew that even though there were competing religious claims on the issue of slavery -- some found biblical sanction in it -- we would still have to choose and decide who we are.

As Americans killed each other, he observed: "Both read the same Bible and pray to the same God. ... The prayers of both could not be answered."

We have many Americans today who read the same Bible but see the truths that define this country very differently. And of course, we have Americans who do not see the Bible as relevant to those truths at all and those who would claim that there are no truths.

As Lincoln observed, the prayers of all cannot be answered. Unless we're resigned to meaninglessness, we must believe that our future will reflect today's choices.

On the hardest moral dilemma of his day, Abraham Lincoln stepped up to the plate and took a stand. He did not say that it was above his paygrade. And this is what makes Abraham Lincoln very different from Barack Obama.

Each time has its challenges. Americans feel betrayed by what they see as unethical behavior in American business and in Washington. Yet few seem to appreciate that moral problems lie at the root of our faltering economy.

Sanctity of life and sanctity of property are cut from the same cloth of eternal law.

In the view of many, including me, it's this law that defines our free country.

Our new president, who sanctions both abortion and massive government intrusion into our economic lives, sees things very differently.

So let's not pretend these fundamental differences don't matter. How we choose will define our future. As Lincoln said, the nation "will become all one thing or all the other."

Founding Principles

Using the IRS to suppress free speech
Feb. 10, 2014

The latest round of the IRS scandal in which tea party and conservative groups have been selectively targeted for harassment by our tax collection agency is unfolding. This comes in the form of proposed new rules from the IRS regarding the operation of organizations falling under the 501(c)4 provision of the tax code.

These are organizations whose purpose is to promote "social welfare," and therefore their income is tax-free. Because promoting a cause or agenda in our free and democratic country cannot be isolated from political activity associated with that agenda, such activity is permissible by 501(c)4 organizations, as long as politics does not become the main purpose. These are the rules of the game that have existed since 1959. But now the IRS wants to change the game.

The new rules they propose expand the definition of "candidate-related activity" so broadly -- to include voter-education campaigns and grass-roots lobbying campaigns and to forbid even the mention of a candidate in any context 30 days before a primary or 60 days before a general election -- that it would make it impossible for these organizations to function.

The IRS would like us to believe they are just trying to clear up some rules that are too vague regarding how these organizations are allowed to operate. But can it be an accident that these new rules come in the midst of the current scandal in which an IRS official, Lois Lerner, admitted that tea party groups were being targeted for harassment?

It was revealed this week at a House committee hearing, during which new IRS Commissioner John Koskinen testified that an email was found from an IRS official indicating intent to scrutinize 501(c)4 organizations.

How much of this was generated by inappropriate politicized activity within the IRS and to what extent it relates to the IRS taking guidance from higher authority -- like the White House -- remains to be seen. It does defy common sense to conclude that the White House has not been involved in this. IRS activity in pursuit of nonprofit organizations escalated in 2010.

It so happens that in early 2010, in the case Citizens United v. Federal Election Commission, the Supreme Court ruled that the ban on independent political expenditures by corporations violated the free speech provisions in the First Amendment of the Constitution.

And it so happens that funding escalated into 501(c)4 organizations after the Supreme Court lifted this ban. And it so happens that a good deal of this activity has been tea party-related activity.

After the Citizens United decision, the president himself weighed in, expressing his outrage about the decision, indicating his intent to "develop a forceful response to this decision."

To the dismay of our president and those with political agendas at the IRS, our Constitution permits free speech and allows corporations to use funds to express a political viewpoint. So the IRS is now trying to render inoperative the vehicles that often receive and use those funds: 501(c)4 organizations.

It is not an accident that if we look around the world, the one thing that uniformly characterizes un-free nations is lack of free speech. Those who love political power hate those who want to question their power, inform citizens and provide a different point of view.

This is what the current IRS scandal is about. IRS officials, whose job it is to collect taxes, have abused their power to harass those whose politics they do not like. And this is what the current attempt to shut down 501(c)4 organizations is about.

The free flow of information and free speech are the oxygen of a free society. Every freedom-loving American should vigorously push back against this abuse of power by the IRS to stifle free speech.

New Obamacare violations of personal liberty
Aug. 8, 2011

Who could forget that rare moment of honesty during the campaign to pass Obamacare when Nancy Pelosi said, "We have to pass the bill so that you can find out what's in it"?

Now we have it, and almost daily there are new revelations about the staggering extent to which our private lives and individual freedoms have been stomped on.

We learn now that free birth control in the form of contraceptives, morning-after pills and sterilization is part of the grand Obamacare socialist dream-come-true.

The health insurance that Obamacare mandates that all employers provide and that all citizens acquire must pay 100 percent for these birth control products and services, with no deductible or co-pays. Birth control gets more preferential treatment than cancer and heart disease.

Liberals say government should be kept out of your bedroom. What they mean by this is that it shouldn't interfere with what you do there, not that it shouldn't force taxpayers to pay for it.

The provision mandating "preventive services" for women was grafted onto the thousand-plus page bill as it passed through the Senate by Maryland Democrat Barbara Mikulski.

After Obamacare became law, Health and Human Services Secretary Kathleen Sebelius farmed out this general directive to the Institute of Medicine to determine what such "preventive services" should be.

This is cast as an arms-length objective procedure. But in Washington, nothing is objective. There are only interests.

The Institute of Medicine's website says it's "an independent nonprofit organization that works outside of government to provide unbiased and authoritative advice to decision makers and the public."

But this "independent" organization gets 55 percent of its funding from the federal government. And it also gets hundreds of thousands of dollars from the pharmaceutical industry.

So, after months of lobbying by Planned Parenthood, financed in part by the $300 million it gets each year from us taxpayers, the Institute of Medicine offered its "unbiased" recommendations that "preventive services" for women include birth control pills and morning-after pills.

Obamacare is a masterpiece in its achievement of leaving no corner of our personal freedoms unviolated. It hijacks our pocketbook, our autonomy of action and our conscience.

The result is to leave us economically and morally impoverished.

A tiny and narrow exemption is carved out so that nonprofits with a defined religious mission, whose employees and target audience share those same values, are not forced to provide insurance that includes free birth control services.

Liberals are committed to religious freedom as long as those religious values do not conflict with their liberal values.

Meanwhile, what we have is another in the vast universe of new mandated health care entitlements that comprise Obamacare. It is the convoluted logic of the liberal mind to use government power to mandate and subsidize free goodies, to sever all links between individual behavior and its consequences and then claim this will lead to lower costs and more efficiency.

It is no wonder the financial markets have been tanking since the passage of the debt-ceiling bill. That bill simply slaps a Band-Aid on a fiscal rupture that will start gushing red ink as soon as Obamacare kicks in full tilt in 2014.

The perverse truth is that Obamacare, sold by our president and congressional Democrats as fiscally responsible, is exactly the opposite.

The Congressional Budget Office forecasts huge deficits and growing debt, double what they are today, driven primarily by health care spending fueled by Obamacare-mandated entitlements.

Michele Bachmann was onto something by demanding repeal of Obamacare as a condition for increasing the debt limit.

Americans need to sober up. The challenges facing us are formidable.

Repeal of Obamacare is on a growing and most challenging list of things to do.

Why we need conservative judges
July 25, 2005

The characterizations we most commonly hear in contrasting liberal and conservative judges include "activism" versus "restraint" and approaching the Constitution as a "living document" versus focusing on "original intent."

However, I think asking a more fundamental question sheds light on why our society's most vulnerable -- the poor and otherwise disenfranchised -- need conservative judges. We should be asking: "What is the purpose of the law?"

In this sense, I would contrast conservative to liberal approaches as the former viewing the core purpose of the law as individual protection and the latter relating to law as a tool for social engineering.

In the conservative approach, the law we have is a product of the wisdom of the ages, and the only surprises today are how the law might apply in new situations. In a liberal world, we live forever in a social experiment, and our reality is the result of whatever thinking happens to be in vogue among the social engineers.

Using this approach, I hereby declare myself to one and all a conservative.

Citizens don't need their lives defined by others. They need protection. And the vulnerable particularly need protection. Protection means having a legal code with integrity and having judges who see their job as relating to that law to protect people from the unjust encroachment by others. I would say a society of tyranny is one in which it is never clear what the law is and how we are protected. Ironically, this also characterizes a liberal society.

This couldn't have been driven home more clearly than by the Supreme Court's recent eminent-domain decision in the Kelo v. City of New London case. The Fifth Amendment exists because of the appreciation that the purpose of law is the protection of individuals. However, there does exist a social reality. So, indeed, there are situations where if individuals are justly compensated, government may take their property for a pressing public use -- like building a road.

However, creative judges over the years have transformed the sense of what public use is to justify taking property from one set of private individuals and turning it over to another set of private individuals who intend to use the property in a fashion that is more appealing to these judges. In this Connecticut case, that would be commercial development.

It is mind-boggling to think that the Supreme Court has ruled to use the law not to protect individuals, but to evacuate them from their homes so a business can come in and do its thing.

And this decision was carried out thanks to the Supreme Court's liberals. The conservatives voted against it. It says it all that Clarence Thomas wrote a dissenting opinion and that the NAACP was there on his side!

A recent Cato Institute study reports on the magnitude of confiscations that have taken place over the years under so-called "urban renewal" programs. The report cites a study estimating that between 1950 and 1980, about 1 million families -- approximately 4 million individuals -- were displaced from their homes by federally sponsored urban-renewal condemnations, inflicting huge social and economic costs on these communities.

I myself fear for my own family's property. My granddad (who used to say you need two things to stay free: property and a gun) acquired several hundred acres in South Carolina through the sweat of his brow. This man, one generation away from his slave predecessors, struggled and succeeded in getting his few acres on which he could be the free man he longed to be.

Now I fear that our family's legacy is not secure. The government could show up in the night -- in a fashion not all that different from the regime of Saddam Hussein, which our troops have fought and died to derail -- to take away our property. Just compensation? What does that mean? How do you compensate someone for their roots, for the home and land they love?

Apparently, the fund that has been set aside to compensate the 15 holdouts in New London is $1.5 million. Because they were roughly 10 percent of the total lot holders, I would estimate that total compensation for the displacement would be about $15 million. The value we put on freedom is becoming cheaper every day.

However, to return to the general from the particular, this wide-ranging interpretation of government takings is rooted in the same school of thought -- a fundamentally liberal school of thought -- that sees the law as a tool of social engineering rather than a tool for protecting citizens.

The Supreme Court justices who have used our Constitution to justify taking property from one set of private citizens and turning it over to others are the same jurists liberals are in love with because they carry their water on issues like abortion and affirmative action. Both of these issues are, of course, pure social engineering and, in the former case, a departure from using traditional law to protect life and inventing new law to destroy it.

Americans, particularly our most vulnerable Americans, need the protection of law. This is why we need great conservative judges.

Traditional Values

Why pro-aborts oppose free speech
Jan. 20, 2014

It's no surprise why pro-abortion forces in America don't want free speech when it comes to raising awareness about this issue of, literally, life and death.

The more people understand the reality of abortion the more they don't want it as a legal, easily accessible part of American life.

Now, as 650,000-plus pro-life demonstrators are about to arrive in Washington, D.C., for this year's March for Life on January 22, noting in protest the 41st anniversary of the Roe v. Wade decision, the Supreme Court has just heard arguments on a critical case involving freedom of speech and this issue.

Seventy-seven-year-old Eleanor McCullen's challenge to a 2007 Massachusetts law that forbids anyone other than patients and employees to stand within a 35-foot radius of the entrance to an abortion clinic has made its way to the nation's highest court.

Arguments that this prohibition is about the physical safety of women entering these clinics are absurd. There already are federal and state laws that prohibit physical interference with or intimidation of clinic patrons.

This law is aimed solely to abridge the free speech of pro-life activists and prevent them from communicating with women arriving at these clinics. This abridgement of speech is a clear and flagrant violation of the freedom of speech guaranteed in the First Amendment.

What a distortion it is that the pro-abortion contingent has managed to get itself labeled "pro-choice." Choice is about light, not darkness, about knowledge, not ignorance.

Why do those who claim to favor "choice" fight so hard against efforts to assure that women who are considering the horrible decision to extinguish the life they are carrying make as informed a decision as possible?

Unfortunately, this is often driven by elitism and racism.

Abortion clinic clientele are disproportionately poor and disproportionately black.

48

Across the board, poor communities and black communities have been devastated for many years by policies designed by liberal elitists convinced they know what is best for these unfortunate souls.

The abortion clinic is often the last stop in a chain of bad information delivered into low-income communities that creates the government-dependent culture that fosters the never-ending cycle of poverty.

But good information at any stage of the cycle can change things forever. That good information could be a pro-life Christian standing at an abortion clinic.

I wrote a number of years ago about a young black woman named Ebony. When she became pregnant, her boyfriend encouraged her to abort the child. She found little problem in arranging an appointment at a clinic, where they assured her she was making the right decision, because abortion would be "cheaper" than having the child.

But Ebony was uneasy. Sitting up late, she called into a Christian radio talk show where she was referred to a crisis pregnancy center. At the center, she saw her baby via ultrasound and changed her mind. At the center, they helped her birth and provided clothes, food and counseling.

When I wrote about Ebony, her son was 4 years old, and she had no doubt about the correctness of her decision -- a decision made because she had the good fortune to get information.

In 1995, 56 percent of Americans polled by Gallup self-identified as "pro-choice" and 33 percent as "pro-life." The last Gallup poll in 2013 showed 48 percent identifying as "pro-life" and 45 percent as "pro-choice."

As I tour the country to speak at crisis pregnancy centers, I hear the stories of sorrow, regret and guilt from those who went down the one-way street of destroying the child with whom they were blessed.

America cannot be a free country without free speech.

Free speech leads us to a deeper realization that we cannot be a free country without proper respect for life.

Planned Parenthood targets black women
May 4, 2013

In 1854, Abraham Lincoln confronted America's first "pro-choice" senator, Stephen Douglas, in a speech in Peoria, Ill. "Choice" then was about slavery, not abortion.

Douglas sponsored the Kansas-Nebraska Act, which addressed the sticky question of how to deal with the legality of slavery in new territories entering the union. The Kansas-Nebraska Act resolved this by "choice." Residents would vote to decide whether slavery would be legal in their territory.

Lincoln challenged Douglas' "pro-choice" position on slavery. According to Douglas, said Lincoln, "the principle of the Nebraska Bill was very old; that it originated when God made man and placed good and evil before him, allowing him to choose for himself, being responsible for the choice he should make."

No, said Lincoln. "God did not place good and evil before man, telling him to make his choice. On the contrary, he did tell him there was one tree, of the fruit of which he should not eat, upon pain of certain death."

The U.S. Constitution, conveyed by the nation's founders 65 years before Lincoln spoke those words, circumvented the question of slavery, permitting the great paradox of a nation founded on the ideals of freedom, which allowed slavery.

The struggle for racial justice in America -- whether fighting against slavery or fighting for civil rights -- has always been informed by absolute standards of right and wrong, of good and evil, that transcend even the cleverest human mind. Black history is testimony to where we wind up when those standards get lost.

Yet, once again, those standards have gotten lost. And, once again, black Americans are bearing the brunt of the cost of a nation that has lost its moral rudder, this time as a result of wantonly legal and available abortion.

According to the Centers for Disease Control and Prevention, blacks accounted for 35.4 percent of abortions performed in 2009, despite representing, according to the 2010 census, just 13.6 percent of the U.S. population.

Let's not be deluded that this is an accident.

Analysis of 2010 census data by an initiative called Protecting Black Life shows that 79 percent of Planned Parenthood abortion clinics are located in walking distance of minority neighborhoods -- 62 percent within two miles of primarily black neighborhoods and 64 percent that close to Hispanic/Latino neighborhoods.

Planned Parenthood, the nation's largest abortion provider, systematically targets minority women for abortion.

Before the Civil War, there were churchgoing Americans who rationalized slavery by believing that blacks were less than human. This view was legally formalized in the Supreme Court's infamous Dred Scott decision.

It is not surprising that our first "pro-choice" senator supported the Dred Scott decision.

Views echoing Dred Scott help rationalize Planned Parenthood's targeted destruction of black children in the womb.

In 1957, Mike Wallace interviewed Planned Parenthood founder Margaret Sanger and asked her whether she believed in sin.

Sanger, whose racist and eugenicist views are well documented, replied, "I believe the biggest sin in the world is parents bringing children into the world that have disease from their parents, that have no chance in the world to be a human being practically. Delinquents, prisoners, all sorts of things just marked when they are born."

It is a sign of these dismally confused times that it was our first black president, Barack Obama, who, last week, became the first sitting American president to address Planned Parenthood.

In his address, the president did not use the word "abortion" once, nor was there a single reference to the current trial and murder charges against Philadelphia abortion doctor Kermit Gosnell.

You'd think he was addressing Ronald McDonald House, not an organization that provided 333,964 abortions last year, disproportionately on black women.

Black unemployment and poverty rates are almost double the national averages. I suppose Planned Parenthood, with support from our president and $542 million in taxpayer funds, feels it is doing its part to solve this problem.

Sodom in the nation's capital
Nov. 23, 2009

At a time when our country is sick, it shouldn't surprise that one of our sickest places is our nation's capital.

The poverty rate of Washington, D.C., almost 20 percent, is one of the highest in the nation: Its child poverty rate is the nation's highest.

D.C.'s public school system, with a graduation rate of less than 50 percent, is one of the worst in the country.

According to D.C.'s HIV/AIDS office, 3 percent of the local population has HIV or AIDS. The administrator of this office notes that this HIV/AIDS incidence is "higher than West Africa ... on par with Uganda and some parts of Kenya." And the principal way that HIV is transmitted continues to be through male homosexual activity.

Amid this dismal picture, the D.C. city council, perhaps on the theory that serving up another glass of wine is the way to help a drunk, is scheduled to vote on December 1 on whether to legalize same-sex marriage in America's capital city.

Looking at the realities in Washington, D.C., should make clear why George Washington said, "Of all the dispositions and habits which lead to political prosperity, religion and morality are indispensable supports."

But the America that our first president had in mind was very different from the vision of our D.C. government officials.

Washington's America was one in which the point of freedom is to allow man to rise to what he can become. To do this, the greatest challenge he faces is conquering himself -- to rise above his baser instincts, to rise above the many temptations that lead him astray. And to achieve this end, as Washington said, "religion and morality are indispensable supports."

In left-wing America, of which the D.C. government is a poster child, freedom means to indulge every instinct that the tradition and religion of Washington would have us overcome.

Where does it lead? Well, look at D.C.

It is tempting to look at D.C.'s realities and just call this a black thing. And by and large it is.

D.C. is largely black -- almost 60 percent. Its poverty is black poverty. Its public school system serves mostly black children. And its AIDS crisis is mostly among blacks.

But the pathologies that strike the weakest parts of our population most brutally are nonetheless pathologies of the nation.

The Brookings Institution is one of our oldest policy institutes and certainly no bastion of conservatism. But in a recently published volume, Brookings scholars Ron Haskins and Isabel Sawhill point out the centrality of the traditional family to the American dream of opportunity and the centrality of family breakdown to poverty.

Reporting data showing the general breakdown of the traditional American family, they say, "Some claim that anyone who is concerned about these trends is simply out of touch with modern culture; we respond that, if that be the case, then, 'modern culture is out of touch with the needs of children.'"

The Catholic archdiocese of D.C. announced that legalization of same-sex marriage would make it impossible to continue its relationship with the D.C. government and would require termination of the social services it provides to some 68,000 of the city's poor -- including about one-third of its homeless. The reaction of D.C. council member David Catania was essentially "So what?" According to him, "Their services are not indispensable."

Is Catania out of touch with the needs of D.C.'s poor?

No. He just has different priorities. More important to him, and more important to D.C.'s left-wing city council, is advancing moral relativism and the indulgences it feeds.

This is more important to them than feeding the poor or recognizing the values that would get them out of poverty.

It should concern every American as we watch our nation's capital city transform officially into Sodom.

~ ~ ~

PART THREE: The Disease of D.C.

"We're not going to allow anyone to inflict economic pain on millions of our own people just to make an ideological point. And those folks are going to get some health care in this country -- we've been waiting 50 years for it."

Barack Obama, September 2013

"Government is the problem," Ronald Reagan once remarked. Our government is becoming increasingly isolated from its own citizens. Ignoring the vital importance of the rule of law to a free society, too many elected officials subvert the law to suit their own ends without a second thought. They blatantly disregard the will of the people in the name of the common good while leading our country on a path toward destruction. The rest of the country is forced to deal with the fallout from their behavior, an increasingly unstable economy and a polarized world of politics.

Our politicians are more than happy to play political games in Washington while their constituents stay uninformed at home. It is more than clear that what they are doing is simply not working. But the blindly conceited of Washington continue to toy with our country, bribing us with wild promises to reelect them, only for them to continue to waste our money on ineffective programs that reward and increase bad behaviors while enriching themselves and their friends.

This sick cannibalistic government, which has no qualms about gorging itself on its own children, has become an example of everything that is wrong with our country. We are tired of our government's broken promises. But are we complicit in ignoring the obvious by returning incumbents year after year to deliver the goodies we think our neighbors should buy for us?

The growing government tab for irresponsible behavior
March 5, 2007

It is unfortunate that so much of the discussion about how to deal with poverty in our country consists of well-meaning people talking past one another.

To state the problem in its starkest terms, one side sees those in poverty as unfortunate victims of circumstances. The other side maintains that, while granting that circumstances are often beyond our control, every individual must bear responsibility for their own life.

The one thing we do know is that as a nation, we're not handling the problem well. This is clear by the extent to which poverty persists and by the huge amount of funds that we spend to bear the direct and indirect costs of it.

Medicaid, the federally and state funded program designed to pay for the health care of about 45 million of the nation's poor, is a major case in point.

Observing the program is like standing helplessly on the wrong side of a cascading avalanche. You watch it escalate and grow with a sense of inevitability that at some point it is going to take you under.

Spending on Medicaid is now a staggering $350 billion. This is double what it was 10 years ago. The federal portion, which is now more than $180 billion, was $14 billion in 1980.

Aside from the alarms that go off from the growing and massive spending, another fact should set off an alarm. That is, at 22 percent of state budgets nationwide, spending on Medicaid now exceeds state budgets for education.

Recognition of this gets us on one important track for thinking about the problem.

Poor health follows from poverty. And poverty follows from poor education.

There is another important theme.

That is that both the way we deliver education to our poor and the way we deliver health care to our poor are 100-percent controlled by government monopolies.

It all converges in the following way.

Take the case of the new HPV vaccine against strains of the virus that can lead to cervical cancer. I've been writing a lot about this because it drives home so many of the mistakes we are making in how we deal with health care and poverty.

As anyone who has been reading about this knows, most states are struggling with the question of whether to mandate this vaccine for preteen girls.

A report from the chief actuary of the Social Security Administration discusses factors that have led to the drop in birth rates. These include greater use and availability of birth control, more women working, postponement of marriage, increased prevalence of divorce and more women choosing to remain childless.

Not surprisingly, the SSA report ignores the impact of legal abortion. But this is a critical factor. You can look at any chart showing historical fertility rates in the United States and see that it bottoms out after the Roe v. Wade decision in 1973 and stays near those levels.

Because fewer and fewer people are working for every retiree, our current level of taxation is nowhere near covering what the requirements for Social Security and Medicare will be soon.

Meanwhile, although Medicaid is usually thought of as health care for the poor, it's the source of funding for most long-term care for the elderly. Today about 60 percent of Americans in nursing homes and long-term care institutions are being covered through Medicaid.

Just think what this financial burden will look like as the elderly become an increasingly large portion of our population.

It's why projections for the shortfalls in Social Security, Medicare and Medicaid combined have been as high as $126 trillion.

A central premise of Obamacare is forcing healthy young Americans to buy health insurance to subsidize overall premium costs for older and less healthy parts of the population. What happens as the percentage of youth in our population continues to shrink?

It should be clear that it is impossible to separate marriage, children and abortion from the nation's overall economic picture. These so-called social issues underpin the fiscal issues.

A renaissance in American family life -- which entails a restoration of marriage and children as central to our culture -- and a purging of the scourge of abortion could restore a healthy future that today looks so ominous.

Constitutional Boundaries

Understanding what the Constitution stands for is key
Jan. 10, 2011

I salute the Republicans of the 112th Congress for their initiative to restore the U.S. Constitution to its legitimate place of prominence in our public discourse by reading it aloud at Congress's opening session and requiring members to cite constitutional authority when introducing new legislation. It will help highlight that the real debate is about the underlying defining principles of our nation, which the Constitution exists to protect.

Democrats mocking these gestures show their disdain for those underlying principles. When Rep. Henry Waxman, D-Calif., says, "Whether it's constitutional or not is going to be whether the Supreme Court says it is," it's like my saying that whether or not I steal from my neighbor depends on my calculation of whether or not I'll get caught.

The Constitution is our operating manual defining the functions and bounds of our federal government. It was meticulously designed by our founders so that we would have government consistent with the values and principles of our nation.

It's in those values and principles that our "eternal truths" lie -- not in the Constitution constructed to secure them. If the drafters didn't see it this way, they wouldn't have provided provisions to amend and change it.

It's in our increasingly tenuous sense of what the truths are that precede the Constitution, or in the questioning by some of whether indeed there are any eternal truths, that our problems lie.

The purpose of government, stated in the Declaration of Independence, is to "secure" our "rights", including those of "life, liberty and the pursuit of happiness." But how can we understand and use our Constitution if we can't agree on what "life" is or what "liberty" is?

Consider one of the most repugnant decisions to ever emerge from the U.S. Supreme Court: the Dred Scott decision.

The decision relegated blacks to subhuman status and precluded the possibility that they could be considered U.S. citizens protected by the Constitution.

The issue was not whether the Constitution was taken seriously. The issue was how prevailing values dictated an understanding of who people and citizens are. And so, per our Supreme Court in 1857, a class of human beings in our country was relegated to chattel.

The Roe v. Wade decision in 1973, which gave open license to kill our unborn children, stemmed not from indifference to the Constitution, but from how we choose to relate to and define what life is -- or the extent to which we even care.

Recently, a federal judge in California overturned as unconstitutional an initiative passed by California voters to define marriage as between a man and a woman.

Lawyers who supported the suit to overturn the initiative included conservative and libertarian lawyers who would claim to support our Constitution as constructed by our founders. What they don't support is an understanding of the definition of marriage as being between a man and a woman as a pre-existing truth that the state should be free to codify in its constitution.

Supposedly, among the truths our Constitution secures is our right to our private property.

But what can that possibly mean if the federal government can define what health insurance is and force under law every American citizen to buy it?

It is a strange understanding of "life" and "liberty" that would allow this to occur. If government can dictate to this extent how I live and what I do, I begin to feel like they own me. I start feeling like Dred Scott must have felt.

So, yes, let's put the spotlight back on our Constitution.

But let's not lose perspective that our understanding and interpretation of it will be just as good as our agreement on and understanding and appreciation of the underlying values it's there to secure and protect.

Return America to Main Street
April 11, 2011

Although my organization's home office is in Washington, D.C., I log some 150,000 miles a year flying around the country.

Traveling back and forth from the nation's capital provides good perspective on the bold contrast between the realities there and in the rest of America.

Washington is booming today, while working Americans in cities across the rest of our nation struggle to see the economic light of day.

Washington Business Journal reports that, based on their latest annual job growth data from February 2010 to February 2011, D.C. is the No. 1 job market in the nation. The Journal reports unemployment in the D.C. area at 5.9 percent compared to a national unemployment rate that just dropped below 9 percent.

According to the S&P/Case-Shiller Index, the leading index of home prices in the U.S., the latest composite of home prices from 20 cities around the country shows an annual decline of 3.1 percent. Of the 20 cities in the composite, only two showed annual home price increases: San Diego -- barely -- at 0.1 percent, and Washington, D.C., with a solid increase of 3.6 percent.

Yes, Washington is booming, its malls are filled, and the wine flows in our capital's fancy, expensive restaurants. The Democratic regime has been good to Washington.

Although our president famously campaigned about purging Washington of "special interests," I wrote then that this was ridiculous. The business of Washington is special interests. So anyone with an agenda to grow the federal government by definition grows these many special interests. And the data bear this out.

Combined lobbying expenditures in our nation's capital for 2009 and 2010, the first two years of the current administration, were at an all-time high of $7 billion.

Over the course of eight years under the George W. Bush administration, when federal spending increased at the highest rate since the Johnson administration in the 1960s, a little more than $1 trillion was added to annual federal spending. The Obama administration has managed to add on another trillion in less than three years.

Yes, friends, the great sucking sound we hear today is the liberal regime in Washington sucking the living daylights out of this nation.

Almost 80 percent of Americans feel today that the country is on the wrong track. Last November, voters fired one-quarter of the sitting Democrats in Congress in the name of change.

Now, Republicans in Congress, in response to this voter mandate, have tried, in their first shot at the federal budget, to cut $100 billion out of $4 trillion in 2011 expenditures, and Democrats have cried foul.

One hundred billion dollars is wasted in Washington on any given day by the time President Barack Obama, Harry Reid and Nancy Pelosi have finished breakfast.

Democrats have dusted off their predictable talking points. Cutting $100 billion out of $4 trillion is "extreme." Yet, somehow $14 trillion of debt is not.

Pushing to cut $300 million from Planned Parenthood is "ideological," but spending $300 million of taxpayer funds on Planned Parenthood to begin with is not.

And perhaps most pathetic of all: Furloughing "nonessential" federal government workers, when the federal government is taking one-quarter of the American economy, would "harm" economic recovery.

Giving USA, a group that tallies charitable giving, reported that the $303.8 billion in private charity that Americans gave in 2009 marked the largest annual drop since it started reporting this information in 1956.

It's time to return America to Main Street. Main Street should not be strangling while Washington parties. Republicans hear the wheezing on Main Street and want to get the oxygen back to where it belongs.

It's time to get this nation back on track. On this there is no compromise. There is just right and wrong.

Despite liberal howls, SCOTUS Hobby Lobby ruling was right
July 12, 2014

Senate and House Democrats are outraged by the Supreme Court's decision in favor of Hobby Lobby in the firm's lawsuit seeking exemption from the Obamacare mandate that employers provide, free of charge, contraceptives to employees.

Senate Majority Leader Harry Reid called the Supreme Court decision "outrageous," and Democrats have introduced bills in the Senate and the House to overturn the decision.

Why exactly is it that Democrats find it so outrageous that in America religious freedom is respected?

The Religious Freedom Restoration Act, under which the owners of Hobby Lobby sued the federal government, assures that no federal law will substantially burden individuals in the practice of their religion. Paying for contraception would violate the Christian principles of Hobby Lobby's owners.

According to Sen. Barbara Boxer, D-Calif., the Supreme Court has decided that the employer, the boss, has total power to deny critical medical care to their employees.

It has long been a sad irony that liberals, who claim to carry the banner of openness and tolerance, stand for exactly the opposite. The liberal idea of tolerance is "my way or the highway."

Even if we accept the claim that contraceptive use is not about promiscuity, but about family planning, and that this should be provided free, a critical question is whether the only way to accomplish this is for the federal government to force employers to pay for it, and whether forcing employers to pay for contraceptives justifies violating the religious convictions of Christian employers such as Hobby Lobby.

The Supreme Court ruled, correctly, that it does not -- particularly when there are many alternative ways to accomplish the same objective. The court, in its decision, noted that the federal government could directly foot the bill for these contraceptives or have insurance companies directly pay for them.

Even if you believe, as I do, that none of this should be about government or business, and that we should have free markets to deliver to private citizens whatever kind of insurance most appropriately fits their needs, there are still private solutions for delivering free contraceptives for those that feel this is needed.

It is called philanthropy. Americans contributed $335 billion to charities in 2013.

If Boxer or the National Organization for Women really thinks it is critical that a woman get free contraceptives, how about, instead of using the power of government to violate the religious convictions of other private citizens, starting your own charity to raise money to do it?

But speaking about religious convictions, free choice and private initiative seems to violate the religious convictions of liberals. They see only one solution to every dilemma: government force.

Rep. Carolyn Maloney of New York, writing in USA Today, wants to makes this about poor women. She notes, citing Justice Ruth Bader Ginsburg's dissenting opinion in the Hobby Lobby case, that the cost of an IUD is nearly the equivalent of a month's full-time pay for workers earning minimum wage. Similarly, the cost of Plan B (the morning-after pill) is realistically out of reach for millions of low-income women."

Only liberals would suggest that the big issue that low-income women need to contend with is getting others to pay for their contraceptives. The crisis that these women need to contend with is being able to get their children into a decent school and finding a man who is willing to marry them, work and build a family and future together.

The very welfare state policies that these liberals love are exactly what have created the conditions that make achieving these two things so inaccessible to low-income women and perpetuate poverty in these communities generation after generation.

The Supreme Court's decision in favor of Hobby Lobby has made America a little freer. Something to celebrate, unless you are a liberal.

State of Failure

Overreliance on entitlements harms U.S.
Jan. 28, 2013

Journalist Bill Moyers, who worked as an assistant to President Lyndon Johnson, shared memories in a column last year about what his old boss thought of our entitlement programs.

It was under Johnson, who championed the "Great Society" in the 1960s, that a good portion of the runaway government spending we are trying to get under control today originated.

Johnson signed into law Medicare, Medicaid, the War on Poverty programs and the Corporation for Public Broadcasting.

Moyers recounted that for Johnson, Social Security and Medicare "were about a lot more than economics."

He recalls a time when the Johnson administration was supporting retroactive increases in Social Security payments. Moyers said he argued for the increases as economic stimulus. But Johnson called him and said:

"My inclination would be ... that it ought to be retroactive as far back as you can get it ... because none of them ever get enough: That they are entitled to it. That's an obligation of ours. It's just like your mother writing you and saying she wants $20, and I always sent mine $100 when she did. I always did it because I thought she was entitled to it. ... We do know that it affects the economy. But that's not the basis to go to the Hill, or the justification. We've got to say that by God you can't treat grandma this way. She's entitled to it and we promised it to her."

I don't think we could have a clearer picture of Johnson's muddled thinking about his job and the role of government, which contributed so much to the problems we have today.

Johnson's words sound so wonderfully compassionate. But let's get things in perspective.

He saw no difference between his relationship and responsibilities toward his own mother, including sending her his own money, and his responsibilities as president of the United States and the relationship of government to citizens.

There is a world of difference between the appropriate responsibility of parents toward their children and children toward their parents, and politicians deciding on how to spend someone else's money for someone else's children, parents or grandparents.

Johnson didn't seem to grasp or care about the fact that family and government are two entirely different social institutions that serve very different purposes.

So the Johnson administration years marked not just the beginning of many huge government programs that we can't pay for today, but they also marked a major cultural change where government began displacing family and personal responsibility.

It is no accident that as the American welfare state grew, the American family collapsed.

In 1960, 72 percent of American adults were married. By 2010, this was down to 51 percent.

The change is most pronounced among two of today's largest Democratic Party constituencies: youths and blacks. In 1960, 45 percent of Americans between the ages of 18 and 24 were married, compared to 9 percent today. In 1960, 61 percent of black adults were married, compared to 31 percent today.

Means testing, targeted tax increases on the wealthy, raising the retirement age -- all proposed ways to keep Social Security, Medicare and Medicaid going as they are -- all simply grow the American welfare state, increase the dependence of working Americans on government and other taxpayers, and displace family and traditional values with socialism.

This is why Democratic leaders are not stressed out by the entitlements crisis facing us. More socialism in America is what they want.

They are not bothered that slow growth and high unemployment go hand in hand with this socialism.

Republicans won't succeed as an opposition party if they keep tiptoeing around the fact that facing America today is a crisis of vision and values.

They need to stop selling the alternative to welfare as unpleasantness and spending cuts. They need to start selling that restored prosperity will only come with a rebirth of American freedom and the values that go with it.

Paul Ryan's budget is a moral budget
May 5, 2012

House Budget Committee Chairman Paul Ryan, R-Wis., provoked some angry pushback when he claimed that not only is his proposed sweeping revamp of the U.S. budget fiscally sound, but also morally sound.

In a CBN interview, Ryan said he draws inspiration from his Catholic faith.

He argues that the Catholic priority for caring for the poor should focus on helping folks move out of poverty: "Don't make people dependent on government so they stay stuck in their station in life. Help people get out of poverty, out onto life of independence."

Catholics criticizing Ryan don't see it this way. They see him cutting back on welfare programs that focus on the needy.

But this is not a new debate, and it's not limited to Catholics. Those on the left of all religious persuasions have long been criticizing religious conservatives, claiming they're indifferent to poverty and care only about abortion and homosexuality.

It's a critical discussion for our nation today, and Ryan deserves credit for casting his proposed reforms in moral as well as economic terms. It provides the opportunity to challenge today's mistaken conventional wisdom, which holds that morality and economy are separate universes having little to do with each other.

I can speak from personal experience going back to my years on welfare. The intent of federal welfare programs might have been to help the poor, but they caused far more damage than benefit.

When you tell a poor mother that to qualify for her check, she must demonstrate that she is single, not working and has no savings, what are the chances she'll get married, look for a job or put money in the bank? When this goes on for generations, what do you think it does to a community?

It's no accident that in 1960, according to the Pew Research Center, five years before President Johnson signed into law his War on Poverty, 61 percent of black adults were married. By 2008, this was down to 32 percent. In 1960, 2 percent of black children had a parent who had never been married. By 2008, this was up to 41 percent.

Moral problems are intertwined with our other fiscal and economic problems, as well. Consider Social Security, whose Board of Trustees just issued a devastating annual report. Board members project the system going into the red in 2035, three years earlier than predicted last year. The system's long-term unfunded liabilities -- the amount by which projected obligations exceed projected revenues -- add up to $8.6 trillion, more than half the size of the entire U.S. economy.

Discussions about how to fix the system focus on numbers and accounting. But the numbers are symptoms, not causes.

The Social Security payments that current retirees get are from the payroll taxes that those currently working pay. What is driving the system into bankruptcy is the shrinking number of those working per retiree. In 1950, the average was 16.5 workers per retiree. Now it is 2.9, on its way to 2.0 by 2035.

What happened?

One major factor is we're having fewer children. Fertility rates -- the average number of births per woman -- have fallen dramatically. The average U.S. fertility rate, per the United Nations, from 2005 to 2010 was 40 percent lower than during 1950 to 1955.

John Mueller of the Ethics and Public Policy Center argues convincingly the major impact of legal abortion on this dramatic drop in the ratio of those working to retirees.

To solve our national crisis, we need to sort out symptoms from causes. The bankruptcy of our entitlement programs is the symptom.

The cause is a loss of individual freedom and a breakdown of values, personal responsibility and marriage caused by entitlement culture materialism.

Ryan is right to see this in moral terms. We must change, and all change begins with character and personal transformation.

Inner-city schools need political Katrina
Feb. 8, 2010

Secretary of Education Arne Duncan said recently, "Our K-12 agenda can be summed up in one word: reform."

If only it were true. But what Duncan calls reform is indeed putting lipstick on a pig. In this case, the pig is Washington's never-changing formula for solving everything: spending ever-increasing sums of taxpayer money.

"Reform" means generating new ideas about how to spend and coming up with clever new titles for programs.

So today it's called "Race to the Top." Duncan has been handed $4.35 billion, taken out of last year's $830 billion stimulus bill, and was given personal discretion for dispensing it to states that propose education reform ideas that strike his fancy. It's the largest discretionary sum ever given to an education secretary.

This past week 40 states submitted proposals.

How do we know Duncan can identify good ideas? We don't.

He says he likes charter schools and performance pay for teachers. He's open to new colors of lipstick that the pig has not sported before. But a pig is still a pig.

There appears to be not a shred of evidence that funneling more taxpayer dollars through Washington to states improves education. Data compiled by conservative Heritage Foundation analysts show that since 1970, federal spending per student, adjusted for inflation, has more than doubled with no discernible change in test scores.

Now a new study released by the Department of Health and Human Services shows that the Head Start program -- the federal program started in 1965 aimed at getting low-income preschool children prepared for school -- has no impact.

Some $166 billion of federal funds has been poured into Head Start. Yet this new study shows that first graders who have been through the program perform essentially the same as those who haven't.

In response to Texas Gov. Rick Perry saying "no, thanks" to new money with stipulations from Washington bureaucrats, Duncan said, "If states are half-hearted, that's probably not a place where we'll invest."

It says it all that Duncan calls a long and unblemished history of shoveling taxpayer funds into a black hole "investing." Can you imagine any investment banker or venture capitalist "investing" in anything with this kind of track record? Chances are zero.

So why must we tolerate it?

If there were evidence that billions of dollars directed into new spending was going to improve education, we taxpayers might be prepared to be put on the hook. But not only is there no evidence, but the real problems the charade pretends to address just get worse.

It's black and Latino kids who languish year after year in failing public schools as the game goes on.

In normal markets, customers drive the quality of the product. In the case of the public education monopoly, the customers -- kids and their parents -- are pawns in the game. Anything that would give the customers power -- such as school choice -- government and union bureaucrats fight.

The Obama administration, with all its lofty rhetoric about reform, quietly has allowed congressional Democrats to kill the successful Washington, D.C., voucher program. The program has demonstrably given 1,300 inner-city kids a better education in private schools at a third of the cost that their counterparts are getting in D.C. public schools.

Even the liberal Washington Post has editorialized to save the program, as President Obama and Duncan turn deaf ears.

Duncan was chastised for recently saying the "best thing" to happen to education in New Orleans was Katrina. But education has markedly improved there, as parents were given school choice in the wake of the disaster.

The best thing that could happen to inner-city education nationwide would be a political Katrina that would give birth to parental empowerment and school choice.

Entitlements and Other Welfare Frauds

Defining our fiscal crisis is first step
Feb. 22, 2011

The first step in solving any problem is defining the problem correctly. It's here, at step one, where we're already failing in how we're thinking about our nation's fiscal crisis.

Despite the fact that we're talking about an out-of-control federal budget, the problem at its root is not a budget problem. It's a cultural problem that reflects poor decisions we're making about how we use our valuable resources. Until we come to terms with this, these problems are not going to get solved and will only get worse.

If a friend of yours were constantly broke because he spends his paycheck on beer and lottery tickets, you wouldn't tell him he has a budget problem. You'd tell him he has a personality problem.

No different with the nation. The fiscal and economic black hole into which we are being sucked reflects bad thinking and bad decisions.

Like the guy who is broke because of beer and lottery tickets, we know we've got a problem. But we still have a lot of work to do to understand the personality, or cultural, problem that's causing it.

Polling reflects this.

Today only 31 percent of Americans are "satisfied" with the "size and power of the federal government." This is down from 41 percent just two years ago and 50 percent 10 years ago.

But although 70 percent of Americans understand that the federal government has gotten out of control and is getting into our lives where it doesn't belong, when we get down to the specific programs that cause the problem, Americans indicate they still want them.

The elephant in the room is entitlements: Social Security, Medicare and Medicaid. These now total up to $1.6 trillion in spending, or about 45 percent of the federal budget. The $1.6 trillion is projected to double over the next 10 years. We simply can't meet these obligations.

Yet polling indicates Americans don't want these programs cut. Recent polling from the Pew Research Center shows that more than 80 percent of Americans want these programs to stay where they are, or to be increased.

How do we reconcile the paradox that most know that the federal government is out of control yet support the programs that are driving it out of control?

One factor is the way the discussion is taking place.

We're hearing from politicians about the need to make "hard choices." They're defining the problem as keeping the programs the same and making cuts to them.

Naturally, there is resistance by taxpayers to take hits on what they believe are benefits for which they've paid taxes.

But when the problem is redefined to fundamentally change the way we do these things, polls show an openness to change.

Polling done by Pew just last September showed major support for changing Social Security to an ownership program rather than a government tax-and-spend program.

Fifty-eight percent said they support being able to invest a portion of their Social Security taxes in a personal retirement account. Overwhelmingly, younger Americans want to do this. Seventy percent in ages 18-29 support the idea and 63 percent in ages 30-49 support it.

In work done by William Shipman and Peter Ferrara last year, reported in The Wall Street Journal, they calculated what a couple, earning incomes at the national average, would have earned if they could have invested their Social Security taxes in a broad index of stocks over their 45-year working lives from 1965 to 2009.

Despite a 37 percent drop in 2008, they still would have earned 75 percent more than they would have gotten from Social Security.

Perhaps more importantly, it would have been their money, in their own account, for their own use, or passed on to their own heirs.

What we're calling a budget crisis is really a government socialism crisis. This is what needs to be addressed if we're going to have a future.

Obama fast-tracking the nanny state
June 15, 2009

President Obama wants health care reform this year.

He said at a town hall meeting the other day that he won't tolerate "endless delay" and that we probably won't reform health care if we don't do it this year.

Now why is that, Mr. President? Will Congress be on vacation for the remaining three years of your term?

Consider that it's not unusual to take a full session of Congress -- two years -- to pass legislation a fraction of the size and consequence of health care reform. Yet our president is demanding that a bill to overhaul a $2.5 trillion sector of our economy -- one-sixth of it -- be considered and passed in a few short weeks.

It ought to be clear that this is not about taking an honest and sincere look at how to make this a better country and how to do a better job at delivering health care to Americans. It's impossible to look at something this massive and deal with it in such a short time frame.

This is about raw politics. When Obama says that if we don't get "it" done this year we probably won't get "it" done, he doesn't mean reforming health care. He means reforming it the way he and Ted Kennedy want to do it: government-run nanny state health care.

To pull it off, they have to move fast.

First, the White House knows that Obama's honeymoon won't last forever. While his personal approval ratings remain high at 60 percent, his disapproval rating, now at 33 percent, is almost twice where is stood last February. And in the latest Gallup polling, the majority now disapproves of how Obama is handling government spending. So the White House wants action now on health care while their man is still popular.

Second, the White House knows that next year is an election year. It will be far more difficult to get members of Congress to play ball.

Third, they know that the big reason HillaryCare failed in 1993 was that the American people were given an opportunity to look at it and consider it. They don't want to make the same mistake of giving voters a chance to actually understand what is about to happen to them. They know that the more Americans have an opportunity to take a look at the nanny state health care freight train the more likely they will jump off the track.

Breathlessness is a great political technique. Tell voters the world will end if we don't get X passed now.

This is how the $800 billion "stimulus" bill got passed earlier this year. We were flashed images of the Great Depression and told our only hope is the stimulus bill.

Now, three months later, it's clear that our current economy bears no resemblance to the 1930s, that signs of recovery are emerging, and thus far only 6 percent of the $800 billion "stimulus" pot of political lard has been spent.

The trillions in new debt have been piled up at such a dizzying pace in the past few months that Americans are numb. The federal government take from our economy has jumped from one-fifth of it to one-fourth.

Now, Obama and his Democratic colleagues want to layer on a new government health care plan to "compete" with private plans. "Compete" to them means raising taxes a few trillion dollars to provide subsidized insurance, and in some cases free insurance, through a government plan in which all Americans will eventually wind up. It also means putting federal bureaucrats in charge of approving what health care procedures we are permitted.

The health care nanny state freight train is moving. Will we wake up before it's too late?

Se habla entitlement
April 17, 2006

When it comes to matters of economy, I think of myself as libertarian. I believe in free markets, free trade and limited government. But I must confess, our Latino neighbors are challenging my libertarian instincts regarding our immigration conundrum.

The recent pro-immigration demonstrations around the country have been a major turnoff.

There is something not convincing about illegal immigrants demonstrating to claim they have inalienable rights to come here, be here, work here, become citizens here -- and making all of these claims in Spanish.

Hearing "We Shall Overcome" in Spanish just doesn't provoke my sympathies. I don't buy that, along with life, liberty and the pursuit of happiness, our Creator endowed anyone with the right to sneak into the United States, bypass our laws and set up shop. Maybe our immigration laws do need fixing. But this is a discussion for American citizens. In English.

This could be the finest hour for the political left if we really can be convinced that illegal immigration is a right, that those here illegally are innocent victims, and that the real guilt lies with U.S. citizens who believe our laws mean something and should be enforced.

Draping these bogus claims in the garb of the civil rights movement is particularly annoying.

The civil rights movement was about enforcing the law, not breaking it. The Civil War amendments to the Constitution were not getting the job done in what has been a long struggle in this country to treat blacks as human beings. If Americans were kidnapping Mexicans and selling them into slavery here, I might see the equivalence. But these are free people, who chose to come here and chose to do so illegally.

Just considering Mexicans, how can we understand their taking to the streets of our country to demand rights and freedom, when they seem to have little interest in doing this where they do have rights, which is in Mexico? There is no reason why Mexico, a country rich in beauty and natural resources, cannot be every bit as prosperous as the United States.

It's not happening because of a long history of mismanagement, corruption and excessive government.

Although Mexico is a democracy, for some reason Mexicans seem to need to be north of the Rio Grande to get politically active and demand the benefits of a free society.

Last year, the Pew Hispanic Center surveyed adults in Mexico and asked them whether they would come to the United States if they had the means and opportunity to do so. Forty-six percent responded yes. Almost half of Mexican adults said they'd rather live here! When asked whether they would do it illegally, more than 20 percent said yes.

Yet in the current contest for the Mexican presidency, the leading candidate is a leftist former mayor of Mexico City who is polling in the high 30s.

Maybe you can figure out why almost half of Mexican adults say they would rather live in the United States, presumably because of the opportunities our free society affords, yet vote for a leftist candidate who would continue policies in Mexico that choke off any prospect for growth, prosperity and opportunity.

So forgive me for being a little suspicious of the wholesome picture being painted of these folks who are pouring across our border allegedly just to be free, work and maintain traditional families.

Anyone who lives in Southern California, as I do, knows that the Latino immigrant community is far from the paragon of virtue the forces who want to encourage open borders would have us believe. I see much of the same troubling behavior that blacks get tarred with. Much of the gang behavior in Los Angeles, unfortunately, is Latino-related. The L.A. Unified School District is more than three-quarters Latino, with dropout rates at the same alarming 50 percent rate as inner-city blacks. Out-of-wedlock births among Hispanic women approach 50 percent.

Those who want to hoist the banner of the Statue of Liberty, Ellis Island and the American tradition of immigration should remember that when immigrants were passing through Ellis Island at the early part of the last century, the federal government accounted for about 3 percent of the American economy. Today it is 25 percent.

Part of the package deal that comes with showing up in the United States today is our welfare state, as well as our free economy. Illegal status is really a temporary situation, anyway. Illegal immigrants' children who are born here are U.S. citizens. Significant demands are being made on our tax dollars in the way of schools, health care and government services, including law enforcement.

Yes, let's encourage freedom. But freedom is a privilege and a responsibility.

We already have enough people here who think it's all about entitlement.

~ ~ ~

PART FOUR: Poverty & Wealth

"We can't drive our SUVs and eat as much as we want and keep our homes on 72 degrees at all times ... and then just expect that other countries are going to say OK. That's not leadership. That's not going to happen."

Barack Obama

"If you've got a business -- you didn't build that," President Obama declared in an unusual moment of transparency during the 2012 presidential campaign. This statement gives a clear picture of Obama's concept of economics. He is the epitome of blind conceit. Denying that wealth is the result of an individual's hard work and responsible behavior, the president blames it for the poverty in our country today.

But poverty and wealth are two sides of the same coin. On one side, the government plantation, bureaucrats decide who deserves success and redistribute wealth in the name of "equality." Personal responsibility is a concept entirely unknown. Instead, individuals depend on the government to supply their every need and want. When the government inevitably fails to follow through, they point the finger at the very hand that feeds them, those who create wealth. In the end, nobody wins. The rich become poor, the poor remain poor, and the government transforms into an inefficient and corrupt behemoth.

On the other side of the coin, we see the power of the free market. Whether through charter schools, the minimum wage or the privatization of retirement accounts, capitalism generates more wealth and more success. Through hard work and personal responsibility, individuals are able to create success for both themselves and others, achieving more than thought possible.

The solution to poverty never comes from the government. The solution to poverty comes from the individual.

The poor are not poor because the rich are rich
July 30, 2011

A study from the Pew Research Center for the People and the Press reporting a record high wealth gap between whites and blacks should have been labeled "handle with care." Care is needed to examine the complex reality behind the fact that "median wealth of white households is 20 times that of black households. ..."

76

And without care, this information will be abused and misused by those in the race business as another excuse to claim racism and demand exactly what blacks, or any of us, do not need -- more government.

Indeed, the Rev. Al Sharpton has already announced plans for protest in Washington, along with the statement: "For those who think we live in some sort of post-racial society, I have news for you: We're anything but."

For one thing, "median wealth" should not be confused with "average wealth." A median is simply the number right in the middle -- there are an equal number of households with higher and an equal number with lower wealth.

"Average wealth" accounts for the actual wealth of those households and reflects the fact, not reflected in the median number, that there are a good number of well-to-do black households.

So whereas median white household wealth is 20 times higher than median black household wealth, average white household wealth is three times higher than average black household wealth.

The racially tinged headline obscures the deeper reality of what is driving the growing wealth gap. That is that over the period of the study, 2005 to 2009, the gap between those with more wealth and those with less has increased for the whole country.

In fact, over this period, the gap between the most wealthy and least wealthy blacks became more pronounced than the gap between the most wealthy and least wealthy whites.

In 2005, the top 10 percent of wealthy black families represented 56 percent of overall black wealth. By 2009, this top 10 percent represented 67 percent of overall black wealth.

You have to wonder what kind of racial claims Sharpton will make about this.

All this is not to minimize a genuine problem. Far more important than where black wealth stands relative to white wealth is the fact that median, or average, black wealth is far less than it should be.

That 35 percent of all black households have zero or negative wealth (net indebtedness) is dismally sad.

What to do?

If there are any public policy implications, it is not to expand government, but to remove it as an obstacle to black wealth creation.

At the most basic level, black children need to get better education and this means giving black parents the choice to send their children to whichever school they want.

A better-educated black population will mean a higher-income earning black population. But income alone is a limited tool for creating wealth. Wealth is created through savings, investment and entrepreneurship. And blacks lag far behind in each category.

The Pew study shows that the major destruction of wealth from 2005 to 2009 resulted from the collapse of housing prices. Blacks suffered disproportionately because black net worth has been almost entirely in their homes.

The idea of allowing investment in a personal retirement account rather than paying the Social Security payroll tax would be a boon to building black wealth.

But when President George W. Bush suggested the personal retirement account idea, National Association for the Advancement of Colored People Chairman Julian Bond said this was asking blacks "to play the lottery with their future."

A life of government guarantees and controls is not a formula for building wealth. Freedom and capital markets are. Blacks need to decide which they want.

And entrepreneurship must become part of black culture. Blacks need to get that poor people are not poor because rich people are rich.

The formula for more black wealth: less government, more ownership and initiative.

U.S. fiscal policy is detached from reality
Jan. 7, 2013

Here are two ways to think about the "fiscal cliff" deal that just took place in Washington.

You are sitting at dinner and television is on, broadcasting the news. There is one story after another about things you don't want to hear. Recession. Unemployment. You walk over to the TV, turn it off or switch to a sitcom or sporting event and sit back down to finish your meal in peace.

Or, a more personal version.

You take your mail out of the mailbox and see the bills that are due. Without opening the envelopes, you throw them into a desk drawer with vague intention to open them at some point. Or you have voice mails from creditors that you erase and then head out to a show.

There is an inconvenient truth called reality. There are aspects of reality -- things involving behavior and obligations that, unlike a rock falling on your head, can be denied.

Our political "friends" in Washington welcomed in 2013 for us by turning off the TV, by throwing the unopened bills into the drawer, and by allowing Americans to enter the new year under the illusion that something fiscally meaningful has been solved or accomplished.

No one can claim that the problem is lack of information.

Open any newspaper or magazine and there is sure to be at least one report about the spending of our federal government, which now takes almost $1 of every $4 produced by the American economy, or about our trillion dollar budget deficits, to which no end appears in sight, or about our national debt, which soon will exceed the value of goods and services our whole economy produces in a year, or about the shortfalls of Social Security and Medicare, which together is about five times that.

Doesn't seem to matter. Turn off the TV. Throw the bills in the drawer. Everything will work out. Always does.

Supposedly what we want is a growing, prosperous nation.

But symptomatic of being detached from reality is behaving in ways inconsistent with what you think you are trying to do.

Economic growth can be the result when success and risk taking is rewarded and sloth and failure is not.

But part of the spending spree of recent years has involved bailing out and subsidizing failure -- auto companies, banks, green energy.

Yet successful small businesses are punished in this fiscal cliff bill. According to the Wall Street Journal, a 2011 Treasury Department study indicated raising taxes on incomes over $500,000 would affect about 750,000 small business and that, according to one survey during the fiscal cliff talks, 29 percent of small business heads indicated the result would be less hiring and 32 percent indicated they would invest less.

Meanwhile, not working is being subsidized by further extending unemployment benefits, already having been extended to a mind-boggling 99 weeks. This all goes to explain why I was and am opposed to this agreement, which some are celebrating.

That inconvenient truth called reality is something Americans badly need to connect with. If we want all this spending, we need to pay for it. That means everyone. Let's get the real numbers on the table and let's get out our checkbooks.

If you don't want to pay, cut the spending.

In the words of the great 19th century French political economist Frederic Bastiat, "When misguided public opinion honors what is despicable and despises what is honorable, punishes virtue and rewards vice, encourages what is harmful and discourages what is useful, applauds falsehood and smothers truth under indifference or insult, a nation turns its back on progress and can be restored only by the terrible lessons of catastrophe."

The Way Out

Only issue now facing Americans is freedom
Sept. 1, 2012

Political parties throw a lot of glitz at us with their made-for-TV spectaculars, which we call conventions. But the choice facing Americans this year is stark and clear, and these conventions provide no new insights or information.

If you think we're struggling because we don't have enough government, then the Democrats are the party for you. If you think the point of government is to protect individual freedom, and the problem is that it has gone way beyond that, then Republicans are the party for you.

No visual dominates the landscape of our nation's capital like the Washington Monument. Today, however, other than memorializing our first president, it also provides a message about the role and efficacy of government.

Last month, August, marked one year since a 5.8-magnitude earthquake shook D.C. The quake caused cracks in the Washington Monument, which stands at a height of almost two football fields, causing the National Park Service to close it.

A year later, the monument remains in disrepair, shut to the 600,000 annual visitors it usually receives.

The Washington Post reported last January that the monument would be closed until sometime in 2013.

According to that report, the contract to do the repairs would "probably not be awarded until late summer, with work starting sometime after that." But now the Post indicates repair of the monument may not be complete until sometime in 2014.

In January 1994, Los Angeles was hit with a massive 6.7-magnitude earthquake knocking down two sections of the Santa Monica Freeway.

Initial estimate from the California Department of Transportation was that it would take 12 to 18 months to do the repairs.

Considering the massive potential costs to the local economy of shutdown of sections of the busiest freeway in the world, Caltrans decided to turn loose the time-tested formula for American success: market incentives and individual ingenuity. The agency opened bidding to contractors who would accelerate the repair process, offering incentive bonuses for early completion.

The result: The repairs were completed in less than three months, with the contractors collecting a $14.5 million bonus for finishing 74 days ahead of schedule.

An enduring society must be a free society. Only when free can individuals deal with life's endless surprises in creative and resilient ways. Bureaucracy and government control are guarantees for failure.

Now, sadly, we watch those on Louisiana's Gulf Coast bear the brunt again of a brutal hurricane. Think of the despair that followed Hurricane Katrina. There was no shortage of opinions that New Orleans was done forever -- that it would never recover.

But human resilience, creativity, will and freedom has revived that city.

According to the Bureau of Labor Statistics, the unemployment rate in the New Orleans region is now below the national average.

The Wall Street Journal recently reported on the surge of entrepreneurial activity that has occurred there.

Tax incentives have given birth to a growing, nationally competitive film industry, with music and software design following suit. A failed public schools system has been revitalized, with 80 percent of the schools now charter schools.

Shouldn't it tell us something that Apple, the icon of innovation, once on the brink of failure, is now the most valuable company in history? And that all the major areas where we are having problems are areas controlled or dominated by government?

Americans don't need to watch fancy, carefully produced political conventions to know that one question faces us this year: whether or not we want to be free.

Educational freedom is today's civil rights issue
May 16, 2011

Criminal charges against one single black mother and a conviction of another for sending their children to schools in districts in which they are not residents provide yet more indications of deep-seated problems festering in our country.

Moreover, it makes you wonder about how long it is going to take for blacks to wake up to the real problem of who and what hold up black progress.

In one case, a single, homeless black mother in Connecticut is now charged with larceny for supposedly "stealing" $15,686 in education services because she sent her 5-year-old son to kindergarten in a school district where she doesn't live by using her babysitter's address.

Earlier this year, a single black mother in Ohio was convicted and sentenced to 10 days in jail and three years probation for using her daughters' grandfather's address so the girls could attend better and safer schools.

Did these women break the law? Technically, yes. But I would call this the 2011 version of the Fugitive Slave Act.

Today's educational reality for black kids overwhelmingly keeps them incarcerated in failing, dangerous schools. It's evidence of the indomitable human spirit that, despite horrible circumstances, many poor unmarried black mothers understand the importance of getting their child educated and will do whatever it takes to get their kid into a decent school.

And yet when they try, they get convicted, jailed, fined, and sent back to the plantation.

The NAACP is working on behalf on the Connecticut mother, questioning the severity and possible racial implications of the charges.

Supposedly, there have been 26 recent cases of kids removed from this school district because of residency issues, but no criminal charges were filed. Why are there suddenly charges against this particular woman?

Racism? Maybe so, and this should be investigated.

But let's not forget the bigger picture -- that the NAACP has consistently opposed school choice and voucher initiatives and has been a stalwart defender of the public school system that traps these kids and prohibits the freedom and flexibility that these mothers seek.

Let's think about the NAACP mindset that on the one hand defends a black mother for sending her kid to school in a district where she doesn't live -- in this case because she is homeless. But at the same time defends the public school status quo that causes these kinds of problems to begin with.

Slowly, here and there around the country, blacks are waking up to the importance of education freedom.

In Illinois, black pastor and State Senator James Meeks has been fighting for vouchers that would give kids trapped in Chicago's failing schools a way out.

Now being revived by House Republicans, the D.C. Opportunity Scholarship program was initiated by a black mother -- Virginia Walden Ford.

But these cases, unfortunately, have been the exception to the rule.

Generally, black establishment politicians and organizations such as the NAACP have defended government public schools and education status quo and have hurt their own communities.

Nothing contributes more to the growing income gaps in the country than disparities in education, and the impact continues to grow.

In 1980, college graduates earned 30 percent more than those with high school degrees. Today, it is 70 percent more. In 1980, those with graduate degrees earned 50 percent more than those with high school degrees. Today, it is over 100 percent more.

It is Republicans who have championed school choice and vouchers that disproportionately will benefit blacks. Jeb Bush pioneered vouchers as governor of Florida. Now Indiana Governor Mitch Daniels has signed into law a far-reaching voucher bill. Pennsylvania Governor Tom Corbett is trying to do the same.

We shouldn't be returning black children to public school plantations and punishing their mothers. They need education freedom and school choice. This is the civil rights issue of our time.

Lesson in education from Oprah
Jan. 8, 2007

What does a multibillionaire need to do to get some respect? Oprah Winfrey spends $40 million to open a school in South Africa for underprivileged girls and everyone is on her case.

Why so much money? Why all the luxury? Did the school really need a yoga room? And, of course, how could Oprah turn her back on her own backyard and spend all that money overseas?

I can't say that Oprah and I have similar visions of how the world works. When I was working on welfare reform 10 years ago, I did her show and it was quite clear that Winfrey and I are on very different wavelengths.

But now I'm going to defend her.

First of all, it's her money. Unlike many in the entertainment business, Oprah isn't hanging around Washington lobbying for you and me to pay for her pet programs. She isn't even doing Oprah-thons asking us to send in checks.

Oprah made her few billion on her own and she runs her own philanthropy program. It's her money, and it's her business how she chooses to give it away.

It's also eminently clear, as her defenders already have pointed out, that Oprah has given tons of money away in her own backyard.

And, frankly, it's hard to question the fundamental instincts of a self-made billionaire when it comes to investment decisions.

"I became so frustrated with visiting inner-city schools that I just stopped going," she says in a Newsweek story about her new school. "If you ask the kids what they want or need, they say an iPod or some sneakers."

In an interview in USA Today, Winfrey says when she has tried to help kids in this country, "I have failed."

This is not to say that Oprah has a clue about what will work to help these kids. But she sure has a feel for what doesn't. And that is simply going into America's inner cities and giving out money.

Are you paying attention Nancy Pelosi? Barack Obama? Black leaders around the country who relentlessly defend a failing status quo despite reams of evidence that we need to do something different?

If we're really looking to be critical about how money is spent, how about a little more attention on those who spend other people's money rather than on those who spend their own.

Yes, of course, I'm talking about the government and those dear politicians who look out so carefully for our welfare.

Who knows how Oprah's school in South Africa will fare?

But could she possibly waste any more money on education than our own government does?

How about our Department of Education, with a budget of $90 billion this year? DOE got started in 1979, compliments of President Carter, with a budget of $14 billion. Anybody out there think our kids are doing six times better on tests?

Despite appropriations for elementary and secondary education that are, in real dollars, more than 50 percent higher today than in 1980, reading scores for 9-year-old kids are virtually unchanged.

Clayton Christensen of Harvard Business School, and author of the highly acclaimed book "The Innovator's Dilemma," makes the point that real change and improvement come from "disruptive technology rather than improvements on the existing system."

That is, when things aren't working well, you've got to look for fundamentally different approaches to the problem at hand.

This is exactly what the political establishment and the teachers' unions fight to prevent in education. It's because their goal is not to deliver the best possible product to their customers, the kids, but rather protection of their own interests. Innovators whose goal is the best possible product will try anything to achieve that end, that goal, that very best result.

Our education establishment has little interest in anything other than asking for more money to do more of the same. They may pay lip service to improvement. But, as we know, actions are the measure, not words. When those in control refuse to be open to all options to strive for the best, it's clear that the best is not the goal.

Vouchers and school choice are the disruptive technology that we need in education. Oprah picked up her marbles and left when she was unhappy. Why shouldn't kids and parents be able to do the same thing?

The Case for Capitalism

Social Security reform is key to closing wealth gap
Aug. 31, 2013

One potential benefit that can come from last week's March on Washington 2013, which commemorated the 1963 civil rights event, is the various data publicized about the current state of economic affairs of black America vis-a-vis the rest of the country.

In particular, it has been an eye-opener for many to see how little progress has been made over the last 50 years in closing the economic gap between blacks and whites.

I call shining light on the data a "potential" benefit because there is no benefit if real remedial action is not taken to improve the state of affairs.

According to data from the Pew Research Center, the gap in median household income in 2011 between blacks and whites was about $27,000 -- $39,760 for black median income and $67,175 for white median income. In 1967, this income gap between blacks and whites was about $19,000. It's grown by $8,000.

The gap in median household net worth between blacks and whites in 2011 -- $91,405 for white median net worth and $6,446 for black net worth -- was about $85,000. This was up from a difference of about $75,000 in 1984, the first time this data was collected.

As we approach 50 years from passage of the Civil Rights Act in 1964, isn't it time for some new thinking? Shouldn't black Americans be asking what could be done to achieve some real economic progress?

There are many factors dragging blacks down economically. But one very straightforward policy change can be made that would have immediate wealth-creation benefits for blacks and all low-income Americans.

It's something I've written about many times. Personal retirement accounts.

According to a Pew Research Center study on wealth gaps between ethnic groups, in 2009, 80 percent of whites had an IRA, Keogh, 401(k) or thrift savings account. Only 41 percent of blacks did.

One can argue that with far less income available, blacks don't have the resources to invest long term in these wealth-building accounts. And because so many don't, blacks tend to understand these savings plans less, which creates discomfort and bias on their part.

These are exactly the reasons why low-income Americans should be given the option to opt out of Social Security and use the funds they are forced to pay in taxes to invest in a genuine wealth-building retirement account.

Let's recall that Social Security is not an investment program. It's simply a tax on current workers that's used to make payments to current retirees.

Social Security takes 12.4 percent annually from just about every income earner. The employee pays 6.2 percent directly, and their employer contributes the other 6.2 percent.

In 2010, the Wall Street Journal published a study by analysts William Shipman and Peter Ferrara that analyzed what an average-income earning couple would have accumulated over a 45-year working life if they could have put that 12.4 percent of their income in an investment account instead of paying Social Security taxes.

They assumed the couple retired in 2009, right after the stock market crashed, and they used actual historical stock performance data for the 45 years from 1965. Even with the big market drop, their savings could have paid out about 75 percent more than they would have gotten from Social Security.

We should also be aware that Social Security taxes are paid up to $113,700 in income. After that you are free. So Social Security is clearly biased against wealth accumulation of lower-income individuals.

We can expect that liberals will start screaming if anyone proposes to allow low-income earners any choice -- even an option -- to get out of Social Security and invest in a retirement account.

Black Americans can listen to them and watch their income and wealth stagnate for another 50 years as the wealth gap continues to grow.

D.C. politicos block Wal-Mart, help special interests, hurts the poor
July 21, 2013

Why, when nothing has created more wealth and eradicated more poverty than capitalism, do left-wing politicians hate it so much?

After all, it's supposed to be the left that care about the poor.

The latest chapter in this ongoing saga of economic perversity is action being taken in Washington, D.C., to prevent Wal-Mart from opening stores there.

The District's council has passed a bill, awaiting signature by the mayor, specifically targeted to block Wal-Mart. It raises the District's minimum wage 50 percent to $12.50 per hour, but only for stores with more than $1 billion in sales and store size of more the 75,000 square feet.

Unionized stores in the District with these characteristics are exempt. In other words, the bill protects special interests and blocks who politicos don't want -- Wal-Mart.

Wal-Mart promptly announced that if the mayor signs the bill into law, they will cancel plans to open three stores, each of which would create around 300 new jobs.

Wal-Mart's "low prices every day" business strategy is one of the greatest success stories in American history.

Opening its first store in 1962, Wal-Mart today has sales of almost a half a trillion dollars, putting it number one on the Fortune 500 list.

According to the company, it now has over 10,000 stores around the world, employs 2.2 million people, and serves 245 million customers per week.

Is anyone forced to shop at Wal-Mart? Of course not. Is anyone forced to work at Wal-Mart? Of course not.

This mind-boggling growth happened as result of freedom. Wal-Mart's huge success is 100 percent the result of delivering products that people freely choose to buy.

Critics of Wal-Mart claim that the company doesn't pay enough. The company responds that its average pay is at or above the industry average.

But the real issue is, what is it the business of politicians what Wal-Mart pays? Unlike government, that fines you or jails you if you don't do what lawmakers want, people work at Wal-Mart because they choose to do so.

Wal-Mart says it gets anywhere from 10,000 to 25,000 applications for 300 to 400 job openings when it opens a store. That's more than 25 applicants per job.

Doesn't appear to me like Wal-Mart has trouble convincing people to work there.

Washington, D.C., is more than 50 percent black. Its unemployment rate is above the national average. Its poverty rate is above the national average.

Yet politicians in Washington D.C. would rather have no new jobs at $12.50 per hour than 900 new jobs at $10.00 per hour.

Some claim that big discount stores like Wal-Mart go into cities and displace small businesses. This is a claim. There is no definitive study that proves this claim.

But again, even if it were true, it would only be true because free people choose it to be so. What business is it of politicians to tell free people where to shop? What business is it of politicians to deprive people the freedom to go to a store that sells them products at the lowest prices they can find?

Low-income earners, the ones that supposedly the left-wing politicos care about, happen to appreciate Wal-Mart's low prices.

One thing I appreciate about the Wal-Mart where I shop, is the greeters.

They are often disabled and other hard-to-employ individuals. Wal-Mart gives them a chance to work.

Capitalism has been the great success it has because it rewards creativity and hard work.

Socialism has been a failure because it deprives freedom, stifles creativity, encourages envy and covetousness, and it rewards sloth and corruption.

American success is about the miracle of freedom. When freedom is displaced by political power, everyone suffers. In this case in Washington, D.C., where politicians are blocking Wal-Mart, those who will suffer the most are the poor.

Don't raise the minimum wage
June 18, 2012

The late Sen. Daniel Patrick Moynihan famously observed, "Everyone is entitled to his own opinion, but not his own facts."

It's an admonition not taken seriously by today's political left. It embraces, extols and advocates ideas and policies based on what it wishes were true, regardless of how often and how consistently the ideas have been proven wrong.

Take, for instance, the minimum wage.

Rep. Jesse Jackson, Jr., D-Illinois, wants to again raise the minimum wage -- from $7.25 to $10.00 -- despite an abundance of experience that doing so accomplishes exactly the opposite of what minimum wage advocates claim is their objective: to make low income earners better off.

Why doesn't McDonalds increase the price of Big Macs if it wants to sell more? It's pretty obvious that consumers will buy less of a product when its price goes up.

So why is it not equally obvious that the consumers of labor -- employers -- will buy less of a class of labor if the price of that labor increases?

The data bears out this simple logic. We have a long history showing correlation between increases in the minimum wage and corresponding increases in unemployment in those sectors that earn in this range -- the young and unskilled.

University of Michigan economist Mark Perry has calculated that over the period of the last minimum wage increase, increasing it from $5.15 in 2007 to $7.25 in 2009, teen unemployment increased 5 percent more than the general increase in unemployment over that period.

Nevertheless, Jackson feels entitled to his own facts. At his press conference announcing a bill to raise the minimum wage, he said, "Now it's time to bail out working people who work hard every day and they still only make $7.25. The only way to do that is to raise the minimum wage."

Ron Haskins, co-director of the Center on Children and Families at the Brookings Institution, recently testified before the Senate Finance Committee on hearings on poverty.

Among the factors that he identified as the causes of poverty is declining participation in the work force. According to Haskins, between 1980 and 2009, work force participation among males declined from 74.2 percent to 67.6 percent.

However, among young black men, work rates declined from 60.9 percent in 1980 to 46.9 percent in 2009.

How exactly does Jackson think he is helping the prospects for these young black men by making it more expensive to hire them?

Haskins' testimony presents an abundance of facts about our experience with poverty and with government-centered approaches to dealing with it. Experience generally characterized, for those that choose to consider facts, by more and more government spending getting less and less.

According to Haskins, federal government spending, per person in poverty, has tripled, since 1980. The total being spent by all levels of government -- federal, state and local -- per person in poverty is now about $23,700 per person.

Despite the dramatic expansion of government spending on poverty programs over the years, there has been little change in the overall rate of poverty.

What's the key in alleviating poverty? Individual initiative and personal responsibility.

According to Haskins, following three rules reduces the chances of an individual ending up in poverty to 2 percent, and increases to 72 percent their chances of winding up a middle class wage earner.

"Complete at least a high school education, work full-time, and wait until 21 and get married before having a baby."

According to Haskins' research, those violating these three rules have a 77 percent chance of winding up in poverty.

What can government do so that our economy will grow more rapidly and generate more jobs?

Appreciate that government cannot create jobs or wealth. Only private individuals can do that. Government should do its proper job and protect lives and property of citizens and minimize getting in their way so they may work, produce and invest.

Free People Creates Jobs, Jobs, and More Jobs

We need to restore the spirit of capitalism
July 29, 2013

President Barack Obama went to Knox College in Galesburg, Illinois, this week to rearticulate his vision for the American economy and to reassure the American people that, yes, he knows what he is doing.

The president's prodigious political skills are always on display, even in the most challenging circumstances.

He can take dismal reality and spin a positive and optimistic picture that will inspire his supporters.

And no matter how many facts may contradict the claims of the president's vision, that vision never changes, and there never seems a moment when he doubts he is right.

The president reminded the audience that he first spoke there eight years ago as a new senator.

He noted the changes that have taken place. He's now president. He now has gray hair.

But what has not changed is the inside of the man. His views have not budged an inch from those of the young senator of eight years earlier.

According to the *Wall Street Journal*, the current economic recovery "is one of the weakest on record, averaging 2 percent. Growth in the fourth quarter of 2012 was .4 percent. It rose to a still anemic 1.8 percent in the first quarter, but most economists are predicting even slower growth in the second quarter."

Yet the president has no doubt that his policies are right. He ticks off the litany of big government programs that allegedly saved us from economic depression. And, with a slight nod that economic reality is not as rosy as he paints it, he concedes, "We're not there yet."

Perhaps it's again worth recalling the $831 billion stimulus package in 2009 that supposedly would keep unemployment below 8 percent. As unemployment galloped past 10 percent, never was there a hint of doubt from the president that his policies were right.

We're just "not there yet."

Now the president tells us we have to keep big, activist government going to save America's languishing middle class.

But the facts are that the middle class has fared poorly under big government.

As the *Wall Street Journal* reports, median household income -- $51,761 -- remains way below where it was before the recession started -- $56,289 -- and where it was when it began -- $54, 218.

But perhaps most notable in the president's remarks is what he did not say.

A magnificent economic miracle has occurred during this presidency. But the president did not find it worth mentioning because it has nothing to do with government.

Breakthroughs in technology have produced a boom in American energy production. American oil production is up 37 percent over the last two years, reversing 20 years of decline.

As of last March, the United States has become the largest oil producer in the world. Oil imports have dropped to 36 percent of our total oil consumption, down from 60 percent in 2006 and the lowest level since 1987.

No government planner could have ever dreamed of this type of miracle. It was not many years ago we were hearing about the world running out of oil.

According to Obama, we are really dealing with different visions of how the world works. And he's right.

One is driven by government planning -- socialism. The other is driven by freedom and private ownership -- capitalism.

Our president seems to be genetically hardwired to the socialist view. And his portrayal of capitalism is harsh.

But as the new American oil boom attests, it is freedom and capitalism that releases the human spirit, taps human creativity and produces prosperity.

Few things are harsher than a stalled economy. People wanting to work and can't.

Even Barack Obama's charisma is failing to mask the fact that if America is to recover, we need to restore the spirit of capitalism.

Entrepreneurs like Steve Jobs build prosperity -- not politicians
July 23, 2012

I think it's a sport for President Barack Obama to make outrageous statements. He said, "If you've got a business -- you didn't build that. Somebody else made that happen," in a recent campaign trip to Roanoke, Virginia, and then watched Republicans go predictably bananas.

Certainly, the multimillionaire business supporters of the president on Wall Street and in Hollywood know this is absurd. Anyone with the mildest understanding of business and capitalism knows this is absurd.

Yet the president struck at the heart of what makes capitalism tick -- individual freedom and personal responsibility -- without his polling numbers in the week that followed budging, and his re-election probability on Intrade.com actually ticked up two and half points.

We are reaching dangerous critical mass of those in our country who have enough stake in big government -- whether they are employed by it, collecting benefits from it or businesses getting favors from it -- that political protection is commanding a higher premium than freedom.

If Americans want prosperity, we need a grand reawakening to the incontrovertible fact that its source is entrepreneurs unfettered by meddling politicians.

Apple Inc. is now the most valuable company in the world. Its recent stock price puts its valuation at around $560 billion, more than $150 billion more than America's biggest oil company, Exxon Mobil Corp.

Fifteen years ago, in 1997, when Steve Jobs returned as CEO of Apple, the company was worth less than $3 billion, about half a percent of what it is worth today. Estimates then were that Apple was several months away from bankruptcy.

John Lilly, a former Apple employee, now a Silicon Valley venture capitalist, blogged after Jobs' death about a talk that Jobs gave to employees shortly after his return. Apple was losing money, its stock was languishing, there were rumors about the company being acquired, and Jobs was asked about a suggestion that the company should just shut down.

He concluded his response with: "If you want to make Apple great again, let's get going. If not, get the hell out." The blogger continues, "I think it's not an overstatement to say that just about everyone in the room loved him at that point, would have followed him off a cliff if that's where he led."

In the following year, according to the account in "Steve Jobs," Walter Isaacson's book about the entrepreneur, some 3,000 employees were laid off and Jobs reviewed Apple's entire product line, pruning it from 15 products to four.

Now Apple is the most valuable company in the world, with innovative products no one would have dreamed of in 1997.

In September 1997, Apple had 8,437 full-time employees.

Today, according to its website, Apple has 70,000 employees worldwide, of which 47,000 are in the United States. The company estimates that 514,000 jobs have been created as a result of employment at Apple, at companies supported by Apple and the economy created by Apple products.

Suppose, when Jobs revamped and shrunk Apple's product line, he needed employees to vote in order to get rid of each product? It, of course, would have been impossible.

But this is what we have when government goes where it doesn't belong, getting into the business of providing retirement services, health care, housing and education. Even if programs work for a while, times inevitably change. Businesses can adjust. Government can't. Changing Social Security, Medicare, Medicaid, public education and government housing policies is about politics, not good economic decisions.

So we're stuck pouring billions we don't have into programs that don't work.

Capitalism is not about being "on your own," as we hear so often from liberals. It's about entrepreneurs, like Steve Jobs, being free to create prosperity by serving their fellow citizens with innovative ideas and products.

And it's about government doing its proper job -- protecting life and property -- so this can happen.

Government is the problem
April 2, 2012

What are the ramifications if the Supreme Court finds the individual mandate provision of the health care reform law unconstitutional? This provision requires individuals to purchase government-defined health insurance or pay a fine.

I hope it will serve as a wake-up call to a nation that is still sleeping through a crisis.

Liberal and open-ended interpretation of the Constitution has rendered it practically meaningless, opening the door to steady growth of the federal government and its inexorable encroachment in our lives over the last half century. The problems we are having today all originate here.

Even if Obamacare is repealed, health care remains a major problem. Costs keep escalating because there is no real, functioning marketplace. Ninety percent of health care expenditures are made by third parties: government, employers and insurance companies. All due to direct or indirect government controls.

Our growing burden of taxes and government debt stems from the growth of government programs that are enabled by open-ended interpretation of the Constitution.

Our private economy, in which freedom and the creative spirit are still allowed to operate, is going great.

A miracle is taking place in energy, with new domestic production of oil and gas made possible by new drilling technologies.

Oil imports, as a percentage of our overall domestic oil consumption, have dropped almost 25 percent since 2005. In North Dakota, where much of this new oil production is happening, production has increased from 10,000 barrels a day in 2003 to 400,000 barrels a day.

Natural gas production has increased 26 percent since 2005, producing U.S. natural gas prices that are the lowest in the world. As a result, according to University of Michigan economist Mark J. Perry, firms that use natural gas -- like chemical and fertilizer businesses -- are actively talking about returning to the United States.

New technologies abound, with more and more gadgets appearing at lower and lower prices.

Computer equipment that cost $1,000 in 1997 today would sell for about $65, Perry calculated.

So why are we turning over more and more of our lives to the most unproductive, least-efficient part of our country: government?

Just over the last four years, government spending has increased from 20 percent of the American economy to 25 percent.

The result is the most sluggish economic recovery since the Great Depression. It is a sign of the American people's depressed spirit that an unemployment rate of 8.3 percent is viewed as good news. This is almost two and half points higher than the average unemployment rate in our country from 1948 to 2010.

But while we suffer, Washington parties.

The unemployment rate in the Washington, D.C., metropolitan area is 5.7 percent. The District's 2.7 percent population growth last year was the highest in the nation, according to demographer Joel Kotkin.

He reports that the capital region's economy expanded 14 percent since 2007. Over the last decade, 50,000 new jobs in the federal government bureaucracy were created, and local federal spending increased by 166 percent.

No wonder in a recent Gallup poll, residents of greater Washington, D.C., expressed the highest level of confidence in the U.S. economy among the nation's largest metropolitan areas.

Isn't it time to turn this around? Why are Americans still tolerating this?

If we are going to get the nation back on track, we've got to get our resources out of Washington and back into the private sector where they can be used creatively and productively. This is how to create jobs.

~ ~ ~

PART FIVE: Where We Stand

"Now are there people who aren't' going to vote for me because I'm black? Absolutely. But I do not believe those are people who would have voted for me, given my political philosophy, even if I were white."

Barack Obama, October 2007

Our politics are divided, our culture is a battleground, our government is sick, and the government plantation is destroying our country. So where does this leave us?

The country can go one of two ways: bigger government and moral implosion, or return to the Judeo-Christian foundation that made us great. Liberal progressives have made their opinion on the matter quite clear. These self-serving blindly conceited are like 2-year-old children that will jump into a swimming pool although they don't know how to swim. Nowhere in history have ideas of socialism, communism, or totalitarianism worked, but so what? Why let facts get in the way of their utopian desires?

Republicans, however, find themselves fighting their conservative base so to not rock the boat of the blindly conceited. Keep your head low, and maybe it will go away.

And so the Republican Party must make a decision: either to continue on their path towards Washington bureaucracy and insider politics, allowing America to slide totally into a Welfare State; or to partner with conservative and tea party Americans to return our nation to the principles of freedom and personal responsibility that once made the Republican Party great.

The former is a path toward self-destruction, the "way of the Whig;" the latter, a road map for returning the United States to wholeness and boldness and exceptionalism.

The tea party and social conservatives have made it clear which decision the decent, law-abiding, responsible people of America want. The question is, will the Republican establishment join with them to help reach their goals?

Which way will the Republican Party go? Which way will the country go? The answers to both questions will become clear soon enough.

Obama showing blacks how big government failed them
Aug. 20, 2011

The election of our nation's first black president is delivering an unexpected message to our black population. Blacks are discovering that what a man or woman does is what matters, not the color of his or her skin.

It seems ridiculous to point out that this was supposedly the point of the civil rights movement. Purge racism from America. But blacks themselves have been the ones having the hardest time letting it go.

It is not hard to understand why black Americans were happy that a black man was elected president of the United States. It was a final and most grand announcement that racism has finally been purged from America.

But for the highly politicized parts of black America, this was certainly not the only message. Because, for the highly politicized parts of black America, the point has always been to keep race in American politics.

For the black political culture that dominated after the civil rights movement, the point was not just equal treatment under the law, but special treatment under the law.

Plus the assumption that more black political power -- defined by more blacks holding office -- would mean that blacks would be better off.

In other words, post- civil rights movement, black political culture embraced an agenda exactly the opposite of what the civil rights movement was about.

Its agenda was to get laws and policies that were racially slanted -- putting individuals in power based on their race rather than their character and capability.

So, according to the script of this political culture, election of a black man as president meant more than an end to racism. If the man holding the highest political office in the nation was black, it must follow that African-Americans would be better off.

Now blacks have a dilemma. We have a black president and blacks are worse off. Not just a little, but a lot worse off. In the words of longtime Congressional Black Caucus member Rep. Maxine Waters, D-California, "Our people are hurting."

Blacks now grapple with two possible conclusions.

One, our black president is a traitor to his race. Our struggles put him in power and now he's not taking care of his folks. He's become, in the words of left-wing professor and activist Cornel West, a "mascot" of Wall Street.

Or, two, that the man's performance reflects his views and his capability, not his race. He's not delivering for anyone. Blacks are hurting more because they were already in worse shape when Obama got elected.

Bad policies hurt the weakest the most.

And it happens that the bad policies that have always failed are those of big government liberalism that have defined modern black politics.

With further thought, blacks might realize it's this same flawed idea -- that growing government and electing black politicians would make blacks better off -- that explains why blacks have remained disproportionately "hurting."

Take the Congressional Black Caucus itself. The average poverty rate in Black Caucus districts is almost 50 percent higher than the national average. Yet, these black politicians have 100 percent re-election rates.

Maybe a real bonus that will have come from electing a black president is that blacks will take seriously Dr. King's dream that we judge men by their character and not their color.

The civil rights movement took blacks to the edge of the Promised Land. But political activism can only remove barriers to freedom. It's up to the individual to embrace freedom and take on the personal responsibilities that go with it.

Maybe blacks will realize that they should blame Obama. Not because he is black, but because he is a liberal. And because he has grown government to the point where the oxygen necessary for freedom and prosperity is being squeezed out of our nation.

The government plantation forever?
March 30, 2010

Let's do a quick thought experiment.

The price of apples keeps going up. The government decides that every American must buy apples. But some can't afford them.

Government starts controlling how much apple farmers are paid; it mandates that every single American buy apples and subsidizes those under a certain income level so they can.

Will the price of apples go down, stay the same or go up? Or, in economists' language, if you limit the supply of a commodity and increase demand, will the price of that commodity go up or down?

Did you say "up"? You get an A. But if you did say "up," you surely are not a Democrat.

Democrats have just committed trillions of our money, and, as a bonus, sold a big chunk of American freedom down the road, betting that everything a college freshman learns in basic economics is not true. Or, that health care doesn't follow the rules of economics. Because our new health care system is pretty much the apple scenario described above.

Or maybe they don't care? Maybe it's not about economics, but instead about ideology and political power. And that the real issue is freedom. They think we've got too much and that politicians should decide what is fair and who should have what.

A revealing moment during the presidential campaign occurred when, during one debate, ABC's Charles Gibson pushed then-Sen. Barack Obama about his stated intent to increase capital gains taxes. Gibson brandished data showing that when you cut this tax, government tax revenues increase, and when you raise it, revenue drops (punishing investment surely produces less).

"So, why raise it?" Gibson asked. Obama responded that maybe it won't happen that way this time. And besides, he said, his motive was "fairness."

After voters in Massachusetts elected a Republican to replace the late Sen. Ted Kennedy, killing the Democrats' filibuster-proof Senate majority, many pundits wrote that President Obama had to move to the political center.

I wrote then that this wouldn't happen because, unlike President Bill Clinton, who was moderate, Obama is a left-wing ideologue. He didn't run for president to be somebody. He did it to do something. He did it to change America.

As polls showed waning public support for what Democrats were pushing on health care, many assumed they would back off. It was conceivable that they could stand rules on their head and ram the thing through using the so-called reconciliation procedure. But why would they do it when polls suggested they would be punished in November elections?

But Obama understood that when you are selling dreams, numbers don't matter.

So, as in the housing and financial debacle we just went through, you commit taxpayer money to subsidize a product to make it look cheaper than it is, you get people to buy it, and when it all comes crashing down, it doesn't matter. By then you're long gone.

And, another bonus, as more Americans get herded onto the government plantation -- 30 million more with this new bill -- it's easy to keep them there. So the most likely political outcome going forward is higher taxes and income redistribution to pay for it all, entrenching socialism more.

As I have written before, if you want to know where it all leads, look at our inner cities that were long ago taken over by government compassion. This is our future, my fellow Americans.

Oh, back to the apples. Their prices were rocketing to begin with because government was already controlling and regulating them.

Republicans are mad. But will they be able to entice Americans off the ever-growing government plantation? Will they propose and succeed in selling the bold ideas necessary to turn around the basket case we're becoming? We'll see.

GOP or TEA

Can GOP be as ideological as Obama?
May 26, 2014

Talk about Republican Party differences between the establishment and the tea party is taking attention from where it really needs to be focused -- the real issues facing the nation.

With all our differences, Americans agree that we're on the wrong track.

The latest Gallup poll asking, "Are you satisfied or dissatisfied with the way things are going in the United States at this time?" shows just 25 percent satisfied. Even among Democrats, just 35 percent are satisfied.

Lest you think that Americans are chronically unhappy, satisfaction in 2000, when George W. Bush was elected president, was over 60 percent. It then spiraled down for the next eight years, bottoming out at 7 percent at the end of his second term. During the Obama years, this peaked at 36 percent in the early days when many Americans still believed that Barack Obama had something new and positive to offer the country.

The portrayal of tea partiers as crazy ideologues that sprouted suddenly from the grass roots in reaction to Barack Obama is not accurate. The tea party movement expressed dissatisfaction that had already long been fermenting. It was dissatisfaction with business-as-usual in Washington that was key to Obama getting nominated in the Democratic Party and elected president.

The Republican establishment is complicit in the problem because none of today's biggest problems are new. They have been growing and obvious for many years, and Republicans who have held power in Washington, both in the White House and in the Congress have ignored them all.

Barack Obama did not invent the problems with American health care. Costs were going through the roof before he got elected. Tens of millions of Americans were living without insurance before he got elected.

But Republicans did nothing. They were afraid of being bold, of taking on hard issues, of being too ideological.

So Americans elected a president, twice, who was not afraid of being bold, of taking on hard issues and of being ideological.

What Barack Obama did was step on the accelerator of the destructive trends that had been already taking place in the country.

The trend toward growing the welfare state, the trend toward more government interference in private American life and the trend toward interpreting religious freedom as absolute moral relativism.

The issue for Republicans today is whether they can be as clear and principled about who they are as the Democrats.

It is not enough to just talk about spending. All government spending is not created equal. Spending for national defense is a clear constitutional responsibility of the federal government.

According to the Congressional Budget Office, the main source of growth of government spending will be entitlements -- government health care programs and Social Security. By 2038, they will double as a percentage of our national economy.

Spending per student in our public school system has increased 200 percent since 1970, with no change in test scores.

Despite claims that so-called "social" issues are different from economic issues, the evidence is overwhelming correlating poverty, lack of education and lack of upward mobility to growing up in a home without two married parents. Can we continue to delude ourselves that we can have a free, prosperous country when almost half our babies are born to unwed mothers?

As our country ages and there are as many Americans over 85 as there are under 5, can we continue to believe that it doesn't matter that we abort a million babies a year?

Lincoln told America that it couldn't be half slave and half free. It will become all one or all the other.

Tea partiers have been the voice of opposition from the grass roots. The question remains if Republicans will listen and respond with the same boldness to lead in the direction of freedom as Obama and his party has in leading in the opposite direction.

A time for confrontation, not compromise
Sept. 27, 2013

Among the pearls of wisdom conveyed in Ecclesiastes is that everything has its time: "A time to be born and a time to die, a time to plant and a time to uproot ... a time for war and a time for peace."

The founders of the United States drew up a constitution to serve as an operating manual, in its checks and balances, for peaceful, deliberative government.

They understood human nature, and set up a system in which competing interests would have to give in to compromise. Compromise, they understood, is a necessary lubricant for the wheels of government "of the people, by the people, and for the people" to turn and allow us to move forward.

But compromise is meant for those competing interests, not for the core principles of the country that the Constitution exists to protect and secure.

When the principles of our free nation under God are under siege, it is a time for confrontation, not compromise.

The other day I watched a short video of a presentation given at a FreedomWorks event by Rafael Cruz, the father of the young Republican senator from Texas, Ted Cruz, now in the spotlight.

Rafael Cruz is a self-made businessman, an immigrant from Castro's Cuba, and a born-again evangelical Christian pastor.

Usually, when someone cites the Declaration of Independence, they mention its famous opening sentences. But Rafael Cruz, in this brilliant summation of what America is about, quoted the signers' closing words:

"... with a firm reliance on the Protection of divine Providence, we mutually pledge to each other our Lives, our Fortunes, and our sacred Honor."

Take a walk around Washington, D.C., any evening. The fancy restaurants are filled with lobbyists and legislators. Try to find anyone who would pledge his or her life and fortune for anything.

The American government is no longer about doing the business of the people while preserving and protecting the principles of a free nation. The principles of freedom have been drowned out by the power elite -- whether politicians, big business lobbyists, or big media -- who use their influence to feather their own beds.

A Jeremiah-like Ted Cruz, ringing the alarm that things are not OK, is an annoyance to the comfortable establishment. As the class of "haves" protects their interests, they assure a dismal future for our young and our poor. They play while the ship sinks.

There is a no more powerful predictor of economic growth and prosperity than a nation's economic freedom.

The just-published 2013 Economic Freedom of the World Report shows that the United States has dropped from being the world's second-most economically free country in 2000 to No. 17 in this year's report.

Our economic arteries are clogged because of excessive government, and it's dragging us down and ruining everything that made America great.

The Obamacare health care law is just the latest huge incursion into the freedom of private American citizens, in a long process of deterioration.

Every year, the trustees of Social Security and Medicare provide a report showing the dismal financial state of these huge entitlement programs. And every year, the political class in Washington ignores it, not having the courage to fight for real change, while things continue to get worse and worse.

Now big business, unions and Congress are getting themselves exempted out of Obamacare, ready to leave the rest of country to get shepherded into socialized medicine.

But Ted Cruz, like his brave father, Rafael, is putting his life, his fortune and his sacred honor on the line to save our beleaguered country.

When Abraham Lincoln took office, he still believed that slavery could be purged from America through deliberation. But soon it became clear that only war would do it.

America must stand by Cruz and other brave tea party Republicans who understand the message of Ecclesiastes that there is a time for everything, and that today is the time for confrontation.

Tea party is the solution, not the problem
Oct. 7, 2013

Let's get clear about the political realities behind the budget impasse in Washington and the government shutdown.

Nothing captures the distortions being perpetrated more than the headline of a Washington Post column by Anne Applebaum that reads: "The GOP Undermines Democracy."

And, according to President Barack Obama, a "faction" of Republicans (read "tea party") is holding the nation hostage to its "ideological demands."

After all, isn't it true that the health care law is the law of the land? Isn't it also true that it passed constitutional muster before the U.S. Supreme Court? And isn't it also true that we have a president, who champions this health care law, who has been elected twice?

All true.

But it is also true that the brilliant architects of the U.S. Constitution provided many checks and balances and a multitude of channels through which the will of the people may, at all times, be expressed.

The move by the Republican-controlled House to pass a bill to authorize spending for the federal government, but to withhold spending authorization for the health care law, is totally legitimate, appropriate and constitutional.

The Constitution vests the power of the purse in Congress. Here is what James Madison, who drafted the U.S. Constitution, had to say:

"The power of the purse may, in fact, be regarded as the most complete and effective weapon with which any constitution can arm the immediate representatives of the people, for obtaining redress of every grievance, and for carrying into effect every just and salutary measure."

The fantastic news is that the system is working.

Ironically, those like Post columnist Applebaum tell us that Republicans, who are boldly exercising their responsibilities and authority under our Constitution, are undermining democracy.

And, ironically, our president refuses to sit down and negotiate with Republicans who are constitutionally representing popular sentiment. Then he says they are the "ideologues."

As of Friday, the RealClearPolitics.com average of polls showed 51 percent oppose the health care law and 43 percent support it. Little has changed since Obama approved it in March 2010.

Polling then showed 49.3 percent were opposed and 40.1 percent were in favor of it.

Against prevailing public sentiment, Congress passed the 2010 law without a single Republican vote, using parliamentary gymnastics that few can explain today. And yet Republicans are being accused of hijacking the system.

An increasing percentage of U.S. households receive more in government transfer payments than they pay in taxes. The figure rose from 20 percent in 1979 to 60 percent in 2009, according to University of Dallas economist Michael Cosgrove.

With all the crocodile tears about inconvenience that this shutdown may cause some nonessential government workers, real tears should be shed for the massive loss of jobs due to a barely recovering economy, larded down with government, debt and a welfare-state culture.

Stanford economist Edward Lazear has reported in The Wall Street Journal that only 58 percent of our working-age population is employed today, compared to more than 63 percent before the recession.

Last June, Lazear wrote, "At the present slow rate of job growth, it will take more than a decade to get back to full employment defined by pre-recession standards."

A new Gallup poll shows 60 percent of Americans say the federal government has too much power, the highest percentage ever recorded by Gallup.

Obama is intentionally playing to the cracks in the Republican Party. He knows Republican leadership is weak-kneed. But if Republican leaders cave in, the country is lost. We need principled and courageous leadership now.

The tea party is the solution, not the problem.

A Republican House Divide

In America today, mainstream means left
June 16, 2014

Just when tea party obituaries were being sounded around the country, Washington fixture of 42 years, Mississippi Senator Thad Cochran, loses to upstart tea party candidate Chris McDaniel.

And one week later, House Majority Leader Eric Cantor, in the blockbuster of this year's political season, is booted out of office in the Virginia Republican primary by an economics professor from Randolph-Macon College, total undergraduate enrollment -- 1,312 students.

Turns out that reports of the death of the tea party are greatly exaggerated.

According to The New York Times editorial page, when writing about Cantor's defeat, the tea party is "producing candidates who are light-years from the mainstream."

Many continue to harbor and sell the illusion, nurtured by media sources like the Times, and reaching sometimes to even The Wall Street Journal, that somehow there is a "mainstream" in American politics today, and that anyone with strongly held conviction is an "extremist" or "ideologue" and not part of this "mainstream."

But if mainstream means not clearly on one side of the political spectrum or the other, a new report from Pew Research shows that what is supposedly mainstream today is not mainstream at all. The report, "Political Polarization in the American Republic," shows that it is now the minority of Americans who are not clearly on the left or the right.

Only 39 percent of Americans define themselves in the middle, as a mixed bag of liberal and conservative values. The majority of Americans, the other 61 percent, see themselves as on the liberal left or the conservative right. Thirty four percent say they are mostly or consistently liberal and 27 percent say they are mostly or consistently conservative.

Just 10 years ago, 49 percent -- 10 percentage points more ---
defined themselves in the mixed middle.

The New York Times would like us to believe that there is a
mainstream in America today because mainstream means status quo.
And because of the massive growth of government over recent years,
today's status quo means acceptance of a great lurch leftward, which
has already occurred.

It sounds so measured and sober to call a candidate
"mainstream."

But mainstream is not measured and sober.

It means shrugging your shoulders at $17 trillion in federal debt,
$4 trillion in federal spending and a tax code of over 73,000 pages.

In polling reported by Gallup, for 45 years, from 1952 to 1997,
over 80 percent of Americans said there is "plenty of opportunity" in
the country. By last year this was down to 52 percent.

The tea party is not an ideological movement. It is a movement
of decent, hardworking Americans from quiet communities who are
no longer willing to let freedom and opportunity disappear as result
of the massive growth of government and a power-satiated political
class in Washington.

Most of America's Declaration of Independence consists of
listing of the violations of the personal liberties of the American
colonists by the king of England. The founding of the country was
not born of ideology but of the practical realities of individuals
wanting to live free, and finding it harder and harder to do so.

This is what is happening today. And it will only stop when
either Americans at the grass roots re-achieve freedom and the
opportunity that comes with it, or they stop caring about it.

America has no center today. You either accept a left-wing status
quo or you are fighting against it.

Some are saying that Eric Cantor is a conservative.

But given where we are today, a politician, particularly one in a
position of leadership, is seen as either part of the problem or part of
the solution.

Increasingly, after many years in Washington, enjoying the
trappings of power, Cantor grew to be perceived as the former.

Wanted: Leaders with conviction and courage
April 4, 2011

As negotiations in Washington on this year's budget (already halfway into the year that this budget is for) come to a head, the rumor mill points to a Washington-as-usual result. That is, split the differences down the middle.

But as King Solomon taught us, resolving a dispute by splitting the difference is not always a sign of virtue.

Republicans want to cut $61 billion from a budget of almost $4 trillion with a deficit of $1.6 trillion.

Current interest payments on the national debt, some $200 billion, dwarf these proposed cuts that Democrats are labeling "extremism."

From a purely political perspective, there are reasons to expect Republican feet to start turning to clay.

First, Democrats and Republicans know that in the 1995 showdown that resulted in shutting down the government, Democrats and Bill Clinton came up the political winners. Although circumstances are very different today from then, that history certainly looms large in political minds.

Second, it's a good bet that current polling gives pause to many Republicans. Polls show that, although in the abstract Americans are concerned about the size of government and runaway spending and debt, when you get down to specific programs, there is little positive sentiment for making significant cuts in the big areas that would make a difference.

And third, there is a critical difference today between the two parties. Ideological differences pose a much greater internal problem today to Republicans than Democrats.

Republicans have today within their ranks some individuals that actually stand for something. Democrats, who have fair party unanimity in their comfort level to go on growing government and aborting our children forever, relish watching internal Republican tensions and potential splits over principle.

So taking things to the brink is just fine with Democrats. They don't see any big problem to begin with, and by the calculations noted above, Republicans would bear all the political costs.

And they may be right.

Even the Wall Street Journal editors are urging Republicans to compromise, arguing that getting any cuts at all is an achievement these days and that they should move on and gird for the next big battle.

But the key assumption that always enables putting things off until tomorrow is the assumption that there will be a tomorrow.

Or, in the words of Lincoln, "You cannot escape the responsibility of tomorrow by evading it today."

The real question is how deeply every single politician who supposedly represents our interests in Washington believes we are in crisis. How much do they believe that, ultimately, things will go on and be just fine no matter what we do?

The polls that show weakness in public sentiment for real reforms and substantial cuts in government should not be taken by politicians as justification for caving in but as a message for the need for real leadership today.

Too many Americans are just not getting it. And how could they? Most folks are busy with their work and families. How can they possibly understand what lurks behind the huge budget numbers they read about, what sprawling government really means and why it is sucking out our vitality, undermining our freedom and destroying our nation?

Great political role models today are two freshman Republicans from Florida -- Sen. Marco Rubio and Rep. Allen West.

Both have publicly drawn lines in the sand on the budget and debt limit debate, and both have had the courage to speak about entitlement reform despite representing a geriatric state.

Democrats are drawing a target on the back of West, a conservative African-American elected in a liberal white district. West is a man of real courage, driven not by fear but by conviction and patriotism.

Freedom is not an entitlement. Without this kind of leadership, we will be toast.

Must things get worse in order to get better?
Oct. 16, 2006

A survey just released by the Pew Center shows that 51 percent of Democrats are enthusiastic about voting in 2006 as opposed to 33 percent of Republicans. This is almost a mirror image of what the picture looked like in 1994.

A Pew Center poll also shows a precipitous drop in support for Republicans and the Bush administration among white evangelicals. It's now a little over 50 percent, whereas in 2004 it was closer to 75 percent.

Given the realities staring us in the face, none of this is a surprise. I know that these polls reflect the facts accurately just from reading my mail.

Republicans and conservatives are fed up with their party and their representatives. But can it be that anything is better than what we now have?

I've gotten letters telling me that I've sold out because I've written that we should not abandon the Republican Party because at least there is a chance of fixing it. What do we gain by allowing Democrats, who are wrong on everything, to regain power, just to express anger at wayward Republicans?

I'm as mad as everyone else.

I've been arguing for years that although the Bush administration pays lip service to traditional values, it has missed the central point: that limited government is the other side of the same coin as traditional values.

Big government and a moral, traditional and genuinely free society simply cannot go together. It's worth remembering the observation of British historian Lord Acton that "power tends to corrupt, and absolute power corrupts absolutely."

The correlation between the amount of power that we put in the hands of politicians, and the tendency of those politicians to become corrupt, is a human reality, not a partisan one. We can expect it from Republicans as well as Democrats.

Given the failure of the current Republican regime to limit government, and to actually find reasons to grow it, what we're seeing today should come as no surprise.

Nevertheless, I still will argue that we shouldn't take our eye off the ball. Conservatives need to stay focused on what we, and all Americans, need -- traditional values and limited government -- and continue to push positively toward this end. Despair is no answer and will only make things worse.

With all the comparisons to 1994, it shouldn't be forgotten that Republicans ran in 1994 on a positive agenda -- the Contract with America. Americans voted for something in '94.

I'm adding nothing new to point out that there is no Democratic agenda in 2006. There are only Democrats looking for power and trying to grab it by taking advantage of Republican incompetence.

Unfortunately, not a challenge.

We ought to think back further than 1994 and go back to 1976 when Jimmy Carter was elected president. There are a lot of similarities between what is happening now and the picture then.

The country was still traumatized by the aftermath of the Vietnam War, by having a president resign as result of the Watergate scandal and what was then called the "energy crisis."

Carter was elected to bring fresh air to Washington. He sold himself as a man of the people who would bring decency back to Washington, and fed-up Americans voted for him in the hope that he would bring the fresh air that they wanted to breathe.

Unfortunately, like all so-called populists, what Carter really believed in was government and not people. To deal with our energy problems, he created a new Department of Energy. To deal with our education problems, he created a new Department of Education.

Four years later, we had double-digit inflation, 20-percent interest rates, a doubling of energy prices and Americans held hostage in Iran.

The country had to go through even greater trauma than it was in in 1976 in order to open the door for the Reagan era four years later.

Do we have to go through this again? Is the only path to electing Republicans who really believe in traditional values and limited government to throw out the current rascals, lock, stock and barrel, and elect Democrats who will show us how bad things really can get?

There is no question that current Republican leadership has lowered the bar. But let's not forgot just how free this country is. We ultimately get the leadership that we want and are willing to tolerate.

I think conservatives have let our elected Republican officials off too easy these past years by tolerating an excessive growth of government that itself was symptomatic of a problem.

The answer is to get refocused, clarify our principles and fix the party.

The question is if we'll have to do it sitting on the sidelines while the Democrats turn what is bad into what is worse.

Slowing the Socialist Ship in 2014

Challenge today is freedom, not unity
Aug. 2, 2010

Pollsters Doug Schoen and Pat Caddell, both Democrats, took on President Obama in a column in the Wall Street Journal last week, criticizing him for not being true to his campaign promise to unify the country.

"Rather than being a unifier," they say, "Mr. Obama has divided America on the basis of race, class, and partisanship."

They don't see Republicans as any better. They claim that Republicans have just followed the administration in trying to exploit hot buttons of race and class.

"The Republican leadership has failed to put forth an agenda that is more positive, unifying, and inclusive."

Although it seems so warm and cuddly to consider the idea of national "unity," what does this really mean? Particularly, what does it mean in a free country?

Isn't the whole point and beauty of freedom that we recognize differences among us as natural and that we view debate, differences of viewpoint and dissent as healthy? Doesn't the idea of "unity" -- of uniformity -- conjure up images of exactly what this country is not about?

A recent Gallup poll on confidence of Americans in our various institutions shows that far and away the institution that we have most confidence in is our military.

On the most basic question -- our survival and our attitude toward those whose job it is to protect us -- Americans are not suffering from division and ambivalence.

But in contrast to the military, in which 76 percent of Americans express a "great deal" of confidence, in what institution do we show the least confidence?

The U.S. Congress. Only 11 percent of Americans express confidence in our elected Representatives.

Understanding why there is such a world of difference in how Americans view our soldiers opposed to our Congress sheds light on the unity issue.

The first order of business in doing a job evaluation is defining what that job is. Once that is clear, we can determine if it is being done well.

In this regard, we have pretty good clarity regarding our armed forces and what their job is. We may have differences regarding how we use our troops. But that is a civilian question, not a military question.

When the appropriateness of General McChrystal's behavior came into question and he was fired, the outspoken General saluted and quietly exited as a soldier and a gentleman.

But how about the U.S. Congress? Consider your sense of clarity regarding what their job is compared to our military. Consider your sense of what they think their job is.

A little vague? A lot vague?

This is where our problem lies.

America isn't about unity. America is about freedom.

But in order to be free, we've got to have a government that protects life, liberty and property with the same zeal and clarity that our military protects our physical selves.

It's the job of government to enforce the rules by which we live and to perform its various functions consistent with those rules. But our national consensus of what those rules are – what life is, what liberty is, what property is – has become troublingly vague and unclear.

How can we possibly have a government that works when increasingly we don't even know what it is supposed to do? How can we have a government that works when we have so many elected officials that don't know what they are supposed to do?

The question on the table today is not whether Americans will be unified. The question is whether we want to be free.

And if so, do we have the national will to revisit and do what it takes to be true once again to the basic "self-evident truths" expressed so clearly in our Declaration of Independence?

Land of the envious and home of the victim
Dec. 12, 2011

President Barack Obama laid out his vision of America Tuesday in Osawatomie, Kan.

Ours is no longer, in our president's take on things, the land of the free and the home of the brave.

America now is the land of the envious and the home of the victim.

Ours is a land, as our president explains it, where the success of one American comes at the expense of another: Where the poor are poor because the rich are rich. And where the role of government is not to ensure "life, liberty and the pursuit of happiness" but to tax away wealth from those it deems to have too much and determine how to invest our nation's resources.

The president chose to give this speech in Osawatomie because President Theodore Roosevelt, a Republican, spoke there in 1910 and made a plea for more government in American life. How clever.

But in 1910, the federal government was extracting less than five cents from every dollar produced by the American economy.

It was not until the 1930s, except during World War I, that this doubled to 10 cents of every dollar. After World War II, this doubled again, to 20 cents.

Now, after three years under Obama's vision, the federal government takes 25 cents of every dollar produced by the American economy. If we throw in the costs of state and local government, barely 50 cents of each dollar of our economic output remains in the private economy.

But Obama thinks we're languishing because we're still too free.

The idea that "the market will take care of everything" may look good on a "bumper sticker," according to our president, but, in his words, the idea of free citizens and free markets "doesn't work" and "never worked."

Perhaps our president ought to wake from his dream, and our nightmare, and take a closer look at the country he is living in.

According to the Kauffman Foundation, which specializes in studying entrepreneurship, almost all net new jobs created in our country come from firms less than five years old.

Net new job growth in America comes from entrepreneurs. Not from government bureaucrats nor even from corporate monoliths.

This entrepreneurial activity takes place at considerable risk. According to one study from Case Western Reserve University, only 30 percent of new business startups are still operating after 10 years.

Entrepreneurs start and build their businesses with personal savings, credit cards, funds from family and friends, and loans and investments from banks and venture capitalists.

But what entrepreneur will take these risks if there isn't upside as well as downside? Who will do it if success is punished rather than rewarded? If power-seeking politicians decide that certain successful entrepreneurs have become too wealthy?

Our president cannot seem to grasp that freedom and entrepreneurship are not about "doing your own thing" but are the essence of what he calls, "we're greater together than we are on our own."

Businesses grow by competing to serve customers.

It is also not about, to the president's confusion, "making up your own rules." It works when we don't make up our own rules and live by eternal truths, which prohibit theft and protect private property. Our problems start when government stops doing its job to enforce those rules and starts making up its own.

We stand at a critical crossroads today in clarifying the role of government in our free country.

Obama was correct to say that "this is the defining issue of our time."

Whatever solutions Republicans propose to deal with issues like government spending, taxation, health care and education must flow from a core vision of what America is about.

Whoever emerges as the Republican presidential nominee must be ready to offer a dusted-off and clear vision of America that will restore our understanding of and faith in the freedom that made and makes this country great.

Racial divide worse under Obama
Nov. 5, 2012

The headline of a recent article by the Washington Post's Peter Wallsten capsulizes, inadvertently, the supreme paradox of the Obama presidency.

"Obama struggles to balance African America's hopes with the counties as a whole," it says.

The story documents Obama's struggles over the last four years, which continue today, to avoid overplaying his hand as the first black president, yet to also not ignore this fact.

But nowhere does Wallsten note the irony that four years ago many understood the meaning of Obama's election as the beginning of the end of the perception of black America as a world apart from the rest of America.

There was exhilaration that the nightmare was over – finally. That wrongs have been righted, that we can get on with America's business without the ongoing issue of race looming, and that we can stop looking at blacks politically as a special class of Americans.

Yet here we are now at the end of four years of the presidency of this first black president, and attitudes about race seem to have hardly changed at all. There is still the sense that black America and the rest of America are not on the same page and that blacks and the country "as a whole" have different needs and different agendas.

Wasn't Obama's election supposed to have changed all of this?

Not only have racial tensions not improved but the racial divide appears to have widened.

"Win or lose," Wallsten continues, "the electorate that decides his fate Nov. 6 will be far more racially divided than the one that propelled him into the history books."

According to a Gallup poll done last year, the third year of the Obama presidency, the election of a black man as president had little impact on the enormous difference in perceptions of blacks and whites on the need for government activism.

Fifty nine percent of blacks, compared to 19 percent of whites, said that government should play a "major role" in trying to improve the social and economic position of blacks and other minority groups in this nation.

Fifty two percent of blacks, compared to 15 percent of whites, said new laws are needed to reduce discrimination against blacks.

If Barack Obama's election has had little or no impact on improving racial politics or changing the sense that blacks must be viewed as a special political class, what exactly, practically, has it meant?

Rather than making things better, it has really made matters worse.

From the perspective of Democrat-voting blacks, the implication of a black president was not a more racially just America. It was about assuming there would be a man in the White House more prepared to sign off on special political treatment for blacks. To the extent this has not happened, there has been dissatisfaction.

From the perspective of conservatives, tensions have increased because criticism of Obama's big-government liberalism has been spun as racially motivated.

The Obama presidency has not ushered in a new era of racial tranquility because, despite all the hype, it's not what it has been about.

The real tension in America today is not about black versus white but about liberalism versus conservatism.

Liberalism is about government as a political agent, not as a protector of individual freedom. By its very nature, liberalism creates political classes – whether based on race or gender or business interests. Those that get the goodies are happy. Those that pay for them are not. Tensions and animosities get worse, not better.

In the end, we all suffer because giving politicians more power means less growth and prosperity.

Things will never get solved until we finally take "e pluribus unum" seriously – that American diversity can only be finally united through one set of values, under God, that enable freedom, one set of true values for all.

~ ~ ~

PART SIX: Blind Obedience

"War forces men to make choices between two or more evils. It forces even the pious to become worldly in order to live wholly as men."

Michael Van Dyke, The Story of Dietrich Bonhoeffer

Did progressive liberals really believe that they could hide behind the ethnicity of President Obama to secularize and socialize America without a fight?

While things look glim for the decent people in quiet communities of law-abiding and hard-working free Americans, when through his Blind Conceit he declared to all that he would transform America and used America's race history to divide and conquer his opponents, President Obama misjudged and miscalculated the resilience of heartland America to protect their freedom, their constitution, their guns and their God.

Deep in the heart of Tea Party America was a hope that Rush Limbaugh was prophetic in his January 2009 proclamation that "I hope he fails." And deep in their actions was to work toward this end.

Everything our nation's first liberal progressive president has touched has been a disaster: from the Middle East to immigration to health care to homosexual outreach. He has even lost his so-called War on Women battle as abortion is rapidly receding thanks to their poster child Kermitt Gosnell, and it will soon be abolished and illegal and unthinkable in America.

The strategy of the left has always been to keep blacks and other low-wage minorities blind to the chains of secular socialism and suspicious of the Republican right. Because deep down even inside their blind conceit, progressives know that when these voters are empowered with truthful information, liberalism will loosen its grip and progressivism will abate for at least another century. So the next step for conservatives and tea party patriots to protect freedom is to open the eyes of those the chains of secular socialism have hit the hardest and have hurt the most.

Let's not forget that Dr. Martin Luther King was a Christian pastor
Aug. 17, 2013

Purging of Grammy Award winner Donnie McClurkin from performing at a concert commemorating the 50th anniversary of the 1963 civil rights March on Washington and Dr. Martin Luther King Jr.'s "I Have a Dream" speech should serve as yet another wakeup call to Christian black Americans.

McClurkin, a black pastor and gospel music superstar, was asked to step down from his featured performance by Washington Mayor Vincent Gray as result of pressure from homosexual activists.

McClurkin preaches against the homosexual lifestyle from his pulpit and says he himself departed and was saved from this lifestyle through God's mercy.

Political correctness and a militant campaign to delegitimize religion and traditional values in America have become more important than our constitutionally guaranteed rights to freedom of speech and religion.

Let's recall that earlier this year, the Rev. Louie Giglio of Atlanta, selected by President Obama to give the benediction at his inaugural, was asked to step aside when it was found that over a decade ago he gave a sermon decrying homosexual behavior and lifestyle.

Anyone who thinks this is a good thing, or thinks it doesn't matter, simply doesn't care or get what a free country is about.

When King spoke on the National Mall 50 years ago, he said he came to cash in on behalf of black Americans the "promissory note" guaranteeing the "riches of freedom and the security of justice" transmitted in the U.S. Constitution and the Declaration of Independence.

The Constitution's First Amendment guarantees freedom of speech and freedom of religion.

What kind of outrage is it that blacks should be willing to accept, in a ceremony commemorating a signature event in civil rights history, that we witness both abrogation of freedom of speech and freedom of religion?

We live in a free country. Those who don't wish to read the Christian Bible are not forced to read it.

Those who don't wish to live as Christians are not forced to do that, either.

But it is quite another thing when traditional Christian values are used as the reason to blacklist a pastor, particularly from an event commemorating black civil rights.

Let's be aware of the concerted effort on the left to purge from memory that Dr. King was a Christian pastor, inspired by the truth of the gospel, who led an organization called the Southern Christian Leadership Conference.

No reference is made at all to King's Christianity at the new memorial to him on the national mall.

I would argue that it is these very efforts to purge Christian values and replace them with political power that have limited the success and achievement of the civil rights movement.

It is the collapse of black family life, the escalation of crime and disease -- much tied to irresponsible sexual behavior -- that has occurred over the 50 years since the March on Washington that has been so deleterious to black progress.

The civil rights movement was a Christian movement. It is high time that the black pastor, rather than the black politician, return to leadership in black American life. It is time for the Bible, rather than political answers, to define black life.

In a poll done by Zogby International earlier this year, commissioned by BET founder Robert Johnson, 28 percent of blacks agreed and 55 percent disagreed that gay rights are the same thing as rights for African-Americans.

Yet homosexuals have hijacked the civil rights movement. And in doing so, they have interjected the very values that are destroying black communities. Let's take back our movement.

Rebuild black families by restoring the centrality of traditional Christian values to black life. Only support politicians who sign onto this agenda. And give black parents the choice to get their kids out of public schools and send them to church schools.

There is an alternative to the abortion culture
May 18, 2013

With the convictions in the case against abortion doctor Kermit Gosnell -- three counts of murdering live babies and one count of involuntary manslaughter -- abortion is back in the national discussion.

It's pretty clear from the grand jury report that, during Gosnell's 30-plus-year career, he likely murdered hundreds, if not thousands of babies. But because of the difficulty in documenting it all, he was convicted of just three.

Reports now are coming in from around the nation indicating that more Gosnells are out there. The abortion lobby claims that as long as we have tight regulations on abortion, a black market will exist.

Abortion, they argue, is like any product or service that consumers want and government prohibits or over-regulates. If they can't get what they want legally, they will get it illegally.

We also hear that we get Gosnells when government refuses to pay for the abortions of poor women. The Hyde Amendment, they say, which prohibits Medicaid compensation for abortion, makes unsafe abortion inevitable.

Poor women, according to this reasoning, desperate because of an unwanted pregnancy, pressed because regulations and costs make abortion difficult to get, turn to sleazebag doctors, who will do it cheaply, with no regard for the woman, the law or safety.

But it is ironic that those who call themselves "pro-choice" argue that the only alternatives facing low-income women are unsafe abortions done by sleazebags or government-subsidized abortions.

There is another choice, but those who call themselves "pro-choice" don't want women, particularly poor women, to consider this option. This option is called "birth."

When conservatives talk about a culture of responsibility, we're not just talking about the personal responsibility of the individual in trouble. We're talking about the personal responsibility of the rest of us toward that individual.

There are now thousands of crisis pregnancy centers operating nationwide. More than 2,000 are affiliated with either Care Net or Heartbeat International. I maintain a regular active speaking schedule for and consult with these centers.

They work with pregnant women in trouble and provide them the services they need to have their child.

They provide ultrasounds, parental counseling, life-management counseling, help with the physical needs of the mother and child and, if need be, help with adoption services.

Unwanted pregnancies often are the result of loneliness, fear and lack of information. Crisis pregnancy centers deal with all this.

The so-called pro-choice activists have an interesting concept of a culture of responsibility. That is to promote a culture that detaches sex from love and responsibility that minimizes the central importance of family that justifies youth sex, promiscuity and the "hook-up" culture.

In short, a culture that encourages people to relate to each other in the same callous way as it encourages women to relate to the unborn children that often result from it all. Then they want taxpayers, other people, to foot the bill.

Is it any wonder we live in a country in which we are drowning in debt directly as the result of this culture of entitlement?

Planned Parenthood, which rakes in hundreds of millions in the abortion business, actively discourages women from going to crisis pregnancy centers.

On the Planned Parenthood website, it calls these centers "fake clinics ... that have a history of giving women wrong and biased information."

These crisis pregnancy centers are financed and run by committed Christian Americans, where often women, for the first time in their lives, experience love and meaning.

The information they get, that Planned Parenthood calls "wrong and biased," is that life should be chosen over death and that responsibility is a community affair.

It is not a given that we must live in a country of promiscuity, unwanted pregnancies and abortion. We do have choice. We can reprogram the destructive culture that we have created and in which we now live.

The Way to Victory

Hanging out the 'help wanted' sign for new conservative leaders
Dec. 27, 2013

As 2013 comes to a close, it's as good a time as any to do some national soul-searching.

Polls show that nearly three-fourths of Americans say the nation is on the wrong track. Disapproval ratings of our president are lodged above 50 percent.

Clearly, whatever was generating the glow that got the most left-wing president in American history elected twice is starting to fade.

Despite the considerable human experience from around the world that socialism does not work, and the considerable experience in our own country that human freedom and capitalism does work, many Americans bought the left-wing sweet talk and sugar-coated promises from Barack Obama that this time things would be different.

As Obamacare socialism implodes, as every conservative observer knew from day one it would, the American people need alternatives to not just how we get our health care, but to the destructive left-wing vision that has gripped this country over recent years.

And here, the Republican Party leadership needs to shoulder its share of the blame.

Nature abhors a vacuum. It is not enough to know what doesn't work. Citizens need to hear, with clarity, what does work, and this can only happen through courageous, principled leadership.

Leadership, by this standard, from the opposition party, the Republican Party, has been woefully lacking.

Two recent surveys point to the deep confusion among the American people.

A Gallup poll last week reported that 72 percent of Americans identify "big government" as "the biggest threat to the country in the future," the highest percentage since Gallup began reporting this in 1965.

Yet when asked in a Pew Research Center survey, also reported last week, which parts of the federal budget should be scaled back to deal with the deficit, most Americans do not want to touch what is the biggest problem: entitlement spending.

Social Security and Medicare take 36 percent of the federal budget compared to the 18 percent that goes to defense spending. And projections show entitlement spending rapidly growing to take an increasingly larger chunk of the federal budget.

Yet 69 percent of Americans are opposed to taking on Social Security and Medicare to deal with the deficit, and only 40 percent are opposed to cutting the defense budget. Even a majority of Republicans — 62 percent — don't want to touch Social Security and Medicare.

When most Americans feel the biggest threat facing us is big government, yet they do not want to take on the biggest factors driving the growth of government, we have got a problem.

This is a problem that can only be addressed through leadership. And at this writing, that leadership is absent.

Not only is it absent but things are moving in the wrong direction.

The Wall Street Journal reported this week, "Republican leaders and their corporate allies have launched an array of efforts aimed at diminishing the clout of the party's most conservative activists."

Americans desperately need leaders today who will be honest that we cannot go on with Social Security, Medicare and Medicaid structured as they are.

Ideas abound how we can get better and cheaper health care through genuinely free markets. But it will never happen without leaders willing to say it.

And we need leaders who are willing to be honest about the moral collapse of our country. Societies without virtue and personal responsibility cannot bear the burdens of freedom and reap its benefits. Can a free country really live with almost half its babies born to unwed mothers?

We got to where we are today as a result of political leaders who thought American freedom is on automatic pilot.

It's not. Freedom requires eternal vigilance.

Senate Minority Leader Mitch McConnell and House Speaker John Boehner should be on alert that conservatives have just begun to fight. We're hanging out the "Help Wanted" sign for a new generation of principled, conservative leaders.

Religious Americans will keep fighting for traditional marriage
May 17, 2014

In 1831, a French aristocrat named Alexis de Tocqueville arrived in America and spent several years traveling and studying life in the communities of the new nation.

He produced a book called "Democracy in America," which Harvard professor of government Harvey Mansfield calls "at once the best book ever written on democracy and the best book ever written on America."

Tocqueville looked at America with open eyes and saw its strengths and its flaws. He reported with honesty about the human damage caused by slavery. But he also saw the beginnings of a great country in which human potential could be realized through freedom. And he recognized the crucial role that morals and religion play in making this possible.

Tocqueville wrote, "There is no country in the world where the Christian religion retains a greater influence over the souls of men than in America."

nd he wrote, "Of the world's countries, America is surely the one where the bond of marriage is most respected, and where they have conceived the highest and most just idea of conjugal happiness."

As we know, today times are changing. Religion and the institutions of traditional marriage and family are being challenged and, rather than being seen as enablers of our freedom, are now regularly portrayed as obstacles to it.

Since same-sex marriage was legalized in Massachusetts 10 years ago, it has become legal in 17 states and the District of Columbia and is now recognized by the federal government.

The onslaught continues where laws protecting traditional marriage in many states are being overturned by courts and lawsuits are now pending in 30 states.

Even the Bible Belt has been penetrated, and recently, a judge in Arkansas struck down state law protecting traditional marriage.

Public opinion has changed dramatically in a relatively short period of time in favor of legal recognition of same-sex marriage, and this is producing an impression that the battle is over. An article this week in National Journal was headlined "Opposing same sex marriage is a waste of your time."

According to the Pew Research Center, the percentage of Americans favoring legal same-sex marriage has increased to 54 percent today from 35 percent in 2001.

However, despite the argument that "gay rights" is today's signature civil rights battle as racial equality was the civil rights battle of the 1960s, blacks are generally not buying it.

According to the Pew survey, support for legal same-sex marriage among black Protestants at 43 percent indicates that support has increased in this community but remains far below the national average.

A coalition of 100 black pastors in Michigan now stands in vehement opposition to a federal district court ruling in March overturning a voter-approved measure that amended the Michigan constitution in 2004 to define marriage as between one man and one woman.

The pastors, along with other Christian groups, are filing an amicus brief in support of the appeal of the court decision by Michigan Attorney General Bill Schuette.

Blacks, on average, attend church with greater frequency than any other ethnic group in the country. And blacks take Scripture seriously.

It is a no-brainer for many church-going blacks that discrimination because of race is very different from choices in sexual behavior.

Only 32 percent of Republicans, according to Pew, support same-sex marriage legalization. This issue, along with abortion, is not going away as a source of tension in the Republican Party.

Black pastors know first-hand how moral relativism destroys communities. They are not about to buy into it.

Nor are Christian evangelicals who represent a meaningful portion of the Republican Party.

Although most blacks and Christian evangelicals have probably not read the words of Tocqueville, they appreciate the truths that he identified in 1835 about the importance of religious values to American freedom.

This fight is far from over.

Unions, public schools and minority children
March 22, 2010

Speaking a couple years ago about technology and education, Apple CEO and founder, Steve Jobs, said that technology wouldn't matter as long as you can't fire teachers.

"I believe that what is wrong with our schools in this nation is that they have become unionized in the worst possible way," he said.

Jobs likened schools to running a small business, which he said could never succeed if you can't hire and fire.

Reasonable? I think so. Would anyone question that there is no single thing more critical to a nation's future than educating its children?

Yet consider that 88 percent of our children get K-12 education in public schools, and that 70 percent of the teachers in these schools have union-protected jobs.

Gallup has been polling public opinion about unions since the 1930s. Last year, for the first time, less than half (48 percent) of those surveyed approved of unions. Fifty-one percent said unions "mostly hurt" the U.S. economy, and 39 percent said they "mostly help."

The percentage of the nation's private-sector work force that belongs to a union has dropped precipitously. In the 1950s, more than 30 percent belonged to unions. Today it's a little over 7 percent. But in our public schools, the direction is completely opposite. In 1960, about 35 percent of public school teachers belonged to unions, and today it's twice that, at 70 percent.

Is it not counterintuitive that most Americans feel unions hurt us, that we allow increasingly fewer goods and services produced in our private sector to be controlled by unions, but we turn increasingly more of our most precious commodity -- our children and their education -- over to a union-controlled work force?

In an article in the latest edition of the Cato Journal, Andrew Coulson notes that, on average, compensation of public school teachers is about 42 percent higher than that of their counterparts teaching in nonunionized private schools. Yet, according to Coulson, research shows that private schools consistently outperform public schools.

He attributes the higher average wages of public school teachers less to union collective bargaining and more to the political clout of unions to maintain the public school monopoly over K-12 education.

More than 95 percent of the political contributions of the two national teachers' unions -- the National Education Association and American Federation of Teachers -- go to Democrats or to the Democratic Party. Their $56 million in political contributions since 1989 equals that of "Chevron, Exxon Mobil, Lockheed Martin and the National Rifle Association combined."

The main beneficiaries of education alternatives are minority children. Yet, at the state level, unions provide a unified lobbying front to block such initiatives.

A recent Wall Street Journal op-ed reported on the glowing success of charter schools in Harlem: "Nationwide the average black 12th grader reads at the level of a white eighth grader. Yet, Harlem charter students ... are outperforming their white peers in wealthy suburbs."

Yet, in 2009, the New York teachers union successfully lobbied the state legislature to freeze charter school spending and now is pushing to limit penetration of charters in school districts.

Kids in Los Angeles' public schools are overwhelmingly Hispanic and black. According to the Los Angeles Times, "just 39 percent of Los Angeles's fourth-graders are even basically literate." Yet, the Times attribute union lobbying to undermining a recent attempt by the Los Angeles school board to open failing schools to nonunionized charters.

Similarly, unions played a major role in recently killing the successful private school scholarship program in Washington, D.C.

But there's a significant and promising sign that blacks are beginning to fight back. The Rev. James Meeks, founder and senior pastor of the largest black church in Illinois, who is also a Democrat state senator, is taking on the unions. He has introduced a bill opening the door for vouchers for kids in Chicago's public schools.

Of Course Politics is Ugly

McDaniel blows it with blacks
June 30, 2014

Incumbent Republican Sen. Thad Cochran's successful game plan, which drove his run-off victory over Tea Party challenger Chris McDaniel for Mississippi's Republican Senate nomination, was unconventional.

But most incredible was the success of this game plan – to reach out to liberal black churches and get Democrat black voters to turn out and vote for Cochran – despite being executed in broad daylight.

Soon after Cochran lost to McDaniel in the primary, necessitating a run-off because McDaniel fell short of getting 50 percent of the vote, papers reported the intent of Cochran's team to turn out black Democrats to overcome the thin margin by which Cochran lost.

McDaniel knew exactly what to expect. The Cochran campaign told him. Yet he remained a spectator through it all. His counter strategy was no counter strategy and just continued what he was already doing: appealing just to Mississippi's conservative white electorate.

Sitting in the White House today is the most left-wing president in the nation's history, elected twice without winning the white vote. I have written about the demographic changes taking place in the country and the need for Republicans to talk about limited government and traditional values to non-white Americans.

If this is true about the nation as a whole, it certainly is true in a state like Mississippi, whose black population, at 40 percent of the state, is the largest in the nation. Half this black population is poor.

Cochran's forces dumped money into liberal black churches, communicating that he is their champion because of the government pork he'll continue to bring into the state.

But a news flash for McDaniel, which he should know, having served as a state senator, is that not all blacks are liberals. In Mississippi's huge black population are many conservative black pastors who want freedom for their flocks. They know that black poverty is not about government money.

A few of these conservative black pastors in Mississippi are part of the national pastor network of my organization, CURE.

Former NFL star Brett Favre made an ad for Cochran in which he talked about Cochran getting " ... critical funding for our schools."

But in the latest Quality Counts report from the publication Education Week, Mississippi is rated 51st in the nation, among 50 states and Washington, DC, in K-12 student achievement.

The report continues, as reported in the Mississippi Business Journal, that "Mississippi ranked among the lowest 10 states in providing young people a chance for success in life, financing schools and improving teaching."

If the success of Mississippi's schools was about "critical" funding from the federal government, why are they the worst in the nation?

The main victims of Mississippi's dismal schools are black children.

In a Pew Research survey of last October, 25 percent of blacks expressed favorability toward the Tea Party, just 6 points less than whites.

But the McDaniel campaign seemed clueless that there were potential allies in Mississippi's huge black population to counter Cochran's liberal assault.

It is pathetic that some commentators are actually writing that Cochran's government plantation appeal to blacks shows how Republicans can reach this community.

In a scene early in the Oscar-winning film Patton, General Patton, who was sent to take command of the demoralized American troops in North Africa in the early days of World War II, is shown looking through field glasses, watching a tank battle that would become America's first victory in North Africa.

He studied the tactics of his adversary German commander Field Marshall Erwin Rommel. As he watched, Patton bellowed out, "Rommel, you magnificent b------, I read your book!"

Thad Cochran laid it out for McDaniel -- he gave him his book -- but McDaniel chose not to read it.

Political means don't achieve moral ends
Jan. 13, 2014

It's too early to predict where New Jersey Gov. Chris Christie's "bridgegate" scandal will lead.

What did Christie know and when did he know it about actions of operatives in his administration who engineered the closing of key traffic lanes, leading onto the George Washington Bridge outside Fort Lee, New Jersey, as political punishment for a Democratic mayor who did not endorse Christie's reelection?

The lane closings caused horrendous traffic jams that might have caused the death of one elderly woman.

But whichever players in this horrible game of political vindictiveness are implicated, there is an important lesson.

Despite our obsession with political systems and processes, the quality of our lives ultimately flows from the behavior of individual human beings and not from any meticulously designed political system.

The best any political system can do is to assure political freedom. But it cannot assure what individuals choose to do with their freedom and the values that will define their lives.

The more we believe that politics alone can make our lives better, and that moral standards are just private matters with no import on the quality of our national life, the deeper we will dig the hole in which we are burying ourselves.

We just marked the 50th anniversary of President Lyndon Johnson's declaration of "an unconditional war on poverty."

But Johnson's lofty political language about eradication of social injustice and poverty and who the man actually was and how he lived is a study in contrasts.

Johnson biographer Robert Caro, discussing his study of Johnson, said "I'm trying to explain how political power worked in America in the second half of the 20th century, and here's a guy who understood power and used it in a way that no one ever had. In the getting of that power, he's ruthless – ruthless to a degree that surprised even me, who thought he knew something about ruthlessness. But he also means it when he says that all his life he wanted to help poor people and people of color, and you see him using the ruthlessness, the savagery for wonderful ends."

But is it possible? Is it possible for a ruthless, savagely vindictive, profane and immoral man to achieve political power and use that power to make the world better?

I think the War on Poverty itself answers this question.

Johnson achieved the heights of political power and then, in the name of compassion, spent other people's money to buy his vision of what the world should look like.

The end has been expenditures, by some estimates, of some $20 trillion dollars and a poverty rate today hardly different from where it was when Johnson declared his war 50 years ago.

About a year and half after Johnson made his War on Poverty speech, he gave the commencement address at Howard University in Washington, DC, and said:

"The family is the cornerstone of our society. More than any other force it shapes the attitude, the hopes, the ambitions and the values of the child. And when the family collapses, it is the children that are usually damaged. When it happens on a massive scale, the community itself is damaged."

When Johnson spoke those words in 1965, about 70 percent of white adults were married compared to 55 percent today. About 60 percent of black adults were married, compared to 31 percent today. In 1965 25 percent of black babies and 5 percent of white babies were born to unwed mothers compared to 72 percent and 29 percent today.

Johnson's promotion of government as the source of life's answers, and his split between politics and personal morality, contributed mightily to the breakdown of the American family that he knew was vital to our society.

Politics and political rhetoric is no substitute for personal morality. Worth keeping in mind as we watch the scandal unfold in Chris Christie's regime in New Jersey.

A time for truth, not word games
Sept. 24, 2012

Perhaps now, in the wake of the heat that Mitt Romney is taking over the leaked four-month-old "47 percent" video, he can better appreciate the position of Todd Akin, the conservative U.S. congressman from Missouri running for U.S. Senate.

Romney is being accused of writing off "47 percent" of voters as not paying taxes and "dependent upon government," who "believe government has a responsibility to care for them."

Of course, Romney's words, recorded behind closed doors at a fundraiser, were not, as he admitted, well chosen. No candidate would call half the electorate deadbeats.

But when Missouri Senate candidate Akin used the unfortunate phrase "legitimate rape" in answering a question about his pro-life stand, the leadership of his own party pulled the rug from under him, despite his immediate clarification and apology.

Akin had a significant lead over his Democratic opponent, incumbent Claire McCaskill, before his own party wrote him off for his bad phrasing.

Now Democrats are having a field day trying to nail Romney for his bad phrasing.

Only 30 percent of Americans, according to a recent Gallup poll, are satisfied with the way things are going in the nation.

Our nation, dangerously, and many fear fatally, is losing its way.

The greatest concern for all at this critical time should be truth. Not word games.

It is fair to say that at this moment Republicans are in a state of disbelief.

With things this bad, with Americans this dissatisfied, with a president whose performance has been this dismal, how can this presidential race even be close?

Yet it is.

It appears that, in the true spirit of Groucho Marx, Barack Obama has said, "Who are you going to believe -- me or your own eyes?" And half the people are choosing him over their own eyes.

Barack Obama has charisma. Mitt Romney doesn't. And this poses a great challenge to the Republican candidate.

Here is how my dictionary defines charisma: "a special quality of leadership that captures the popular imagination and inspires unswerving allegiance and devotion."

Is there anything Romney can do? I believe there is. The question is if he is willing.

Charisma in a biblical sense implies divine grace. It is the radiance of an individual who connects to and becomes a vessel for divine truth.

However, there are false prophets. And a false prophet, who truly believes his own personally conjured-up vision, can be charismatic.

The only weapon against a false prophet is hard, unvarnished truth.

We have indeed become a government-dependent nation. And we have indeed become a nation in which the sanctity of family and the sanctity of life are widely disregarded.

The growth of government dependency, the displacement of personal responsibility for government responsibility and the unraveling of the American family all have moved in lockstep.

And our moral bankruptcy and fiscal bankruptcy are occurring together.

The fiscal viability of entitlement programs is driven by the assumption that those who work can pay for those who are retired. But as life spans increase while we produce fewer children, as a result of self-centered lifestyles and abortion, our moral bankruptcy produces our fiscal bankruptcy.

The most recent trustees report for Social Security and Medicare shows the unfunded liabilities of these programs at $63 trillion, four times the size of our gross domestic product.

We have a false prophet leading the nation whose only message is "trust me."

Democrats want to play with words and spin while the country is drowning. They are selling the status quo by appealing to natural human fears of change.

Entitlement programs as we have known them must change. Moral relativism mistakenly called freedom must be labeled for what it is.

Republicans need to embrace, not run, from the truth and tell it to the American people. This is a time for truth, not word games.

2016 and Beyond

A new birth of American freedom
July 8, 2013

A Fourth of July Gallup Poll presented an interesting picture of our country.

Americans overwhelmingly express pride in being American, yet the division is wide and deep about what being an American means.

Eighty-five percent of respondents say they are extremely or very proud to be an American.

Yet, 71 percent say they think the signers of the Declaration of Independence would be disappointed how the country has turned out.

Only 15 percent of conservatives and 12 percent of Republicans say the signers of the Declaration would be "pleased" with how the country has turned out. But 41 percent of liberals and 42 percent of Democrats say the signers of the Declaration would be pleased.

Clearly, there are very different ideas between the two parties and between conservatives and liberals about what truths the signers of the Declaration felt were self-evident and what exactly rights to "life, liberty and the pursuit of happiness" means.

That's not to say that there was unanimity of opinion even among those who signed the Declaration of Independence.

To state the obvious, there are signatures affixed to the bottom of the Declaration of men who saw no inherent contradiction in a nation founded on the idea of liberty in which slavery was legal.

My guess is that the 85 percent who today express pride in being an American do so because they believe this is a free and moral country. We all agree, I think, on these principles.

But like the difference of opinion about slavery two centuries ago, we have huge disconnects among large parts of our population about what a free and moral country is about.

Anyone who follows what I write can guess where I stand.

It is hard for me to believe that many in our country see no contradiction in believing that freedom can be an American ideal while half of Americans live in households getting some sort of government benefits.

Or that somehow a country can be thought of as free in which 40 cents of every dollar the national economy produces goes to government at either the federal, state or local level.

Or that government can put us in debt to the tune of the total value of the annual output of our economy.

Or that the real debt burden sitting on the American public is some $90 trillion -- more than five times the size of our gross domestic product -- that represents the unfunded liabilities of Social Security, Medicare and other government programs.

How can we see this as a free, moral country when we legally and casually use abortion as a means of birth control and provide hundreds of millions of taxpayer funds to Planned Parenthood, the nation's largest abortion provider?

Or that government can tell us what kind of health care we need and must buy and can tell employers what kind of health care they must provide.

Or that government can force employers to provide birth control and abortion pills to employees, even, as in the case of the Christian owners of Hobby Lobby, it violates their religious convictions.

Or that our children go to public schools where it is illegal to pray or teach traditional family values.

There's been a lot of writing recently about the Civil War battle of Gettysburg.

When President Abraham Lincoln gave his famous address at Gettysburg, Pennsylvania, in 1863, he said the nation's business was "unfinished," and he defined the task ahead that "this nation, under God, shall have a new birth of freedom."

The challenges to freedom stand before us today as they stood before Lincoln then.

America is deeply divided and confused, as it was when the bloody battle at Gettysburg was fought.

We again need courageous leadership that will lead us back to the path of freedom and moral principle that inspired our founders and is our destiny.

World needs an America that understands freedom
April 25, 2011

At this time when Christians and Jews celebrate Easter and Passover, a near record number of Americans feel religion is losing its influence on American life.

According to Gallup's latest survey, 69 percent now feel that religion is losing its influence on life in our country. This percentage has been trending upward over recent years.

But a far sharper similar trend occurred in the 1960s.

In 1962, 32 percent felt that religion was losing its influence on American life, but by 1970 this increased to 75 percent.

It's interesting that such a large increase in the sense that religion was losing its influence occurred during the 1960s, the period of the civil rights movement. It seems counter-intuitive.

You'd think that the civil rights movement, fueled by moral passion and a driving conviction about the need to fix grave injustices in the country, would have occurred when there was a sense that religion was becoming more, not less, influential in American public life.

How might we think about this?

One way would be to consider that it's a lot easier to see what's wrong, to know what you don't want, than to see what's right and what you do want.

Getting rid of barriers to freedom is a different problem from living as a free person once those barriers are gone.

Blacks didn't want to live in an America defined by Jim Crow and discrimination. But what kind of America did they want?

The America in which Dr. King founded the Southern Christian Leadership Conference was an America that increasingly saw religion as an obstacle to freedom rather than as a framework to enhance and enable it.

The American public square where King and other black pastors marched was an American public square increasingly sanitized from the presence of God and religion.

In 1962, prayer in public schools was found unconstitutional.

By 1973, abortion on demand was legalized.

In 1960, less than 5 percent of American babies were born to unwed mothers. Today, more than 40 percent are.

Pastors in the 1960s held up the Bible as the authority to fight the immorality of discrimination and make the case for equal rights under the law. But they made their case in a nation that increasingly saw redemption in politics and materialism.

The morality of freedom transformed into the politics of race. The antidote of personal responsibility transformed into entitlements and victimization.

We've now gone beyond blacks just buying into the great welfare state lie. We now have a black president who is leading us all into the abyss.

A black president more interested in protecting abortionists than babies, burying the nation hopelessly into debt, piling on more and more spending with increasingly worthless dollars, to pay for government programs that never have and never will work.

This is happening at a time in a world increasingly in chaos. Millions in nations in the Middle East suddenly are aspiring toward freedom and mobilizing to achieve it as blacks did here in the 1960s.

But they are faced with the same dilemma. What does it mean to be free? It's easier to know what you don't want than what you do.

Unfortunately, the spreading chaos in the Middle East is exacerbated by the absence of leadership from an America, once the world's beacon for freedom.

How can those in the Middle East look to us when the American president's message is that the poor are poor because the rich are rich and that eternal moral truths are irrelevant to political freedom?

The world is waiting for a new America to come forth that again understands that freedom isn't about politics but about moral truths and personal responsibility.

Give thanks for American exceptionalism
Nov. 28, 2011

The Pew Research Center has provided some timely food for thought as we enter our traditional holiday season.

According to a recent report comparing attitudes in Europe and America, only 49 percent of Americans now feel that American culture is superior to others. This is down from 60 percent in 2002.

For those that may find this troubling, there is more reason for concern in that only 37 percent of young Americans, aged 18 to 29, say American culture is superior.

What the study does not examine is what we mean by culture.

I happened to hear a discussion on one of the cable shows about this report, and the discussants were bewailing the prevalence of reality shows, Kim Kardashian and Facebook.

But I think this is a misreading of culture. Culture is about the prevailing core attitudes of a society. And, when we look further into this same study, we find that American attitudes are distinctly different from their European counterparts and that these attitudes very much reflect what is uniquely American.

For instance, 58 percent of Americans feel that individual freedom is more important than government "guarantees that nobody is in need." Only 36 percent of French and 36 percent of Germans feel this way.

Only 36 percent of Americans agree that success is largely determined by "forces outside our control." But 72 percent of Germans and 57 percent of French agree with this.

And 50 percent of Americans believe religion is very important in contrast to 21 percent in Germany and 13 percent in France.

Americans are distinct from Europeans in our beliefs in the importance of individual freedom, of personal responsibility and religious faith.

Can it be an accident that these values that are so prevalent in American culture today are in line with the principles stated in the nation's founding document 235 years ago? That our Creator endowed us with rights to life, liberty and the pursuit of happiness and "That to secure these rights governments are instituted among men."

Distinctly American is our credo, but also that being American is defined by free choice and a set of principles rather than blind circumstance of geography or genetics.

To point to the fact that American culture is distinct does not necessarily prove that it is better.

Is it?

Considering economic performance, there is little comparison between our nation and Europe. Per capita GDP, the economic output per each individual in the country, is $47,200 in the United States compared to $32,700 in Europe.

The average per capita GDP in the European Union is less than that of America's poorest state, Mississippi ($32,764).

One hint that there might be something special going on here is that our problem seems to be limiting the number of people who want to come in, rather than preventing people from escaping.

According to the State Department, more than 5 million people are now waiting to immigrate to the United States in various family and employment categories.

Although American attitudes are distinct, they are changing and trending in the direction of Europe. So if you think this is a problem, and I do, there is reason for concern.

I consider my own experiences and know that nowhere else in the world could I live the life I have been living.

Where else could a young black mother on welfare conclude she was on the wrong path, walk away from it, get her degree, build a business and a non-profit organization that includes on its board of advisers a former U.S. senator and attorney general of the United States and a former counselor to the president of the United States and U.S. attorney general?

My work is inspired by my conviction that America is truly exceptional, and I pray every day that we do not lose our way.

~ ~ ~

About the Author

Star Parker is the founder and president of CURE, the Center for Urban Renewal and Education, a 501(c)(3) nonprofit think tank that promotes market-based public policy to fight poverty. She is a weekly columnist, distributed by Morris Communications and other major Internet news sources, with readership up to 8 million a week. Before her involvement in social activism, Star had seven years of first-hand experience in the grip of welfare dependency. After a Christian conversion, she changed her life, and today she is a highly sought-after commentator on national news networks for her expertise on social policy reform. Star's other books include "Uncle Sam's Plantation" (2003) and "White Ghetto: How Middle Class America Reflects Inner City Decay" (2006).

~ ~ ~

CPSIA information can be obtained
at www.ICGtesting.com
Printed in the USA
LVHW080013121120
671417LV00015B/2110